A heat-stroked "dreamache," *The Rendering* renders a digital dustbowl of land
and data over the poet's anger, over pages of apocalyptic ~~
over maps to the extinct and dying. Anth
desert sun does to signage—cracks it open
to expose the blistered surface underneath.
ekphrasis gather here to be shattered by Co
turbulent dread, smoking wreckage at a dead ond or US "ancientfuture."
Certainly, I trust the poet who writes "the annihilation of anything is
exhausting." Even so, this bravura collection asserts that in recording
destruction, Cody can make a stunning warning against it.

- Douglas Kearney

In *The Rendering*, Anthony Cody pays homage to Francisco X. Alarcón
and Juan Felipe Herrera, two of our most important Latinx multilingual
experimentalists who have pushed the poem into new visual and mystical
territories. Yet Cody builds on what these brilliant artists have done by
creating work that is so singular in its vision, that is impossible to classify
or pin down, that is so beautifully complex and miraculous as it mines the
histories of migration and settlement and property and seizure. Here cultural
and environmental devastations and displacements are indexed and mapped
to shape a narrative that is personal, communal, spiritual, lexical, lyrical,
translational, material, multi-modal and off-the-page-virtual. This is mind
blowing art for our past and future apocalypse.

- Daniel Borzutzky

"I confuse today near the Fresno Rescue Mission with 1939" writes Anthony
Cody in *The Rendering*, a book that chronicles and prophesies a past/future,
climate/capitalist apocalypse. With charts and photos, poll questions and
couplets, erasures and digital verse reverb/erations, these poems push into and
against the limits of the archive and the page itself. Cody will teach you new
ways to read and conceive of the lyric as well as to feel history as both ever
present and ever open to potential renovation. "Play the track, two times slow,"
Cody tells us. "The layer of [PAUSE] is an unpaid echo in the mechanics of
site, an elder gustmemory of afternoon." More than a compilation of Dust
Bowl photographs and Depression-era songs (although both form part of
this assemblage), this is a recontextualization, a grand experiment and a great
excavation. *The Rendering* is a fiercely original and wholly indispensable work.

- Susan Briante

THE RENDERING

THE
REN
DER
ING

ANTHONY
CODY

Cover art by Phil Chang
"Replacement Ink for Epson Printers (Matte Black 324308) on Hahnemühle Photo Matt Fibre", 2017, 32.5 x 43.5 in, Unique archival pigment print, www.philchang.com

Cover and interior set in Arial Black and Adobe Caslon Pro

Cover and interior design by Anthony Cody

Printed in the United States
by Books International, Dulles, Virgina
On 50# Glatfelter B19 Antique
Acid Free Archival Quality Recycled Paper

Library of Congress Cataloging-in-Publication Data

Names: Cody, Anthony, 1981- author.
Title: The rendering / Anthony Cody.
Description: Oakland, California : Omnnidawn Publishing, [2023] | Summary: "In a series of experimental ecopoems, The Rendering confronts the history of the Dust Bowl and its residual impacts into our current climate crisis while acknowledging the complicities of capitalism. These poems grapple with questions of wholeness and annihilation in an Anthropocenic world where the fallout of settler colonialism continues to inflict environmental and cultural devastation. Anthony Cody encourages readers to participate in the radical act of refreshing and re-imagining the page, poem, collection, and the self, while intuiting what lies ahead should our climate continue on its current destructive trajectory. The Rendering asks: can wholeness, or a journey toward wholeness, exist in the Anthropocene? And, if wholeness cannot exist in the Anthropocene, then what of the living, once the living have "achieved" annihilation?"-- Provided by publisher.
Identifiers: LCCN 2022057662 | ISBN 9781632431141 (trade paperback)
Subjects: LCSH: Poetry.
Classification: LCC PS3603.O29548 R46 2023 | DDC 811/.6--dc23/eng/20221205
LC record available at https://lccn.loc.gov/2022057662

Published by Omnidawn Publishing, Oakland, California
www.omnidawn.com (510) 237-5472 (800) 792-4957
10 9 8 7 6 5 4 3 2 1
ISBN: 978-1-63243-114-1

hay habrá soy eres somos este futuro vuelto pasado todo lo que hubo

will be I you we are this future turned past all that once was is

Francisco X. Alarcón
"Rueda víbora" / "Snake Wheel"

Contents

In the scrolling, witness
a logging machine annihilate
a tree into parts. This is social

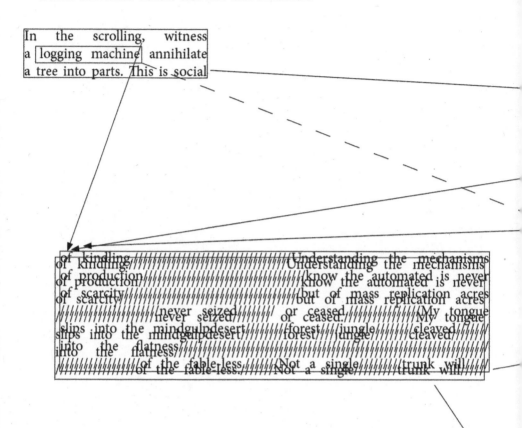

of kindling. Understanding the mechanisms
of production know the automated is never
of scarcity but of mass replication acres
never seized or ceased. My tongue
slips into the mindgulpdesert forest jungle cleaved
into the flatness
of the fable-less. Not a single trunk will

where will whale?

what was bird?

where forest?

what ocean?

where living?

air?

12

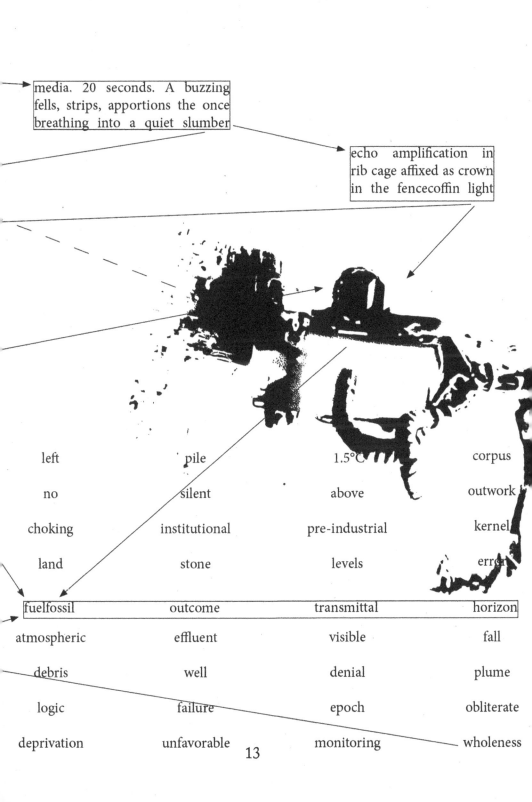

media. 20 seconds. A buzzing
fells, strips, apportions the once
breathing into a quiet slumber

echo amplification in
rib cage affixed as crown
in the fencecoffin light

left   pile   1.5°C   corpus

no   silent   above   outwork

choking   institutional   pre-industrial   kernel

land   stone   levels   error

fuelfossil   outcome   transmittal   horizon

atmospheric   effluent   visible   fall

debris   well   denial   plume

logic   failure   epoch   obliterate

deprivation   unfavorable   monitoring   wholeness

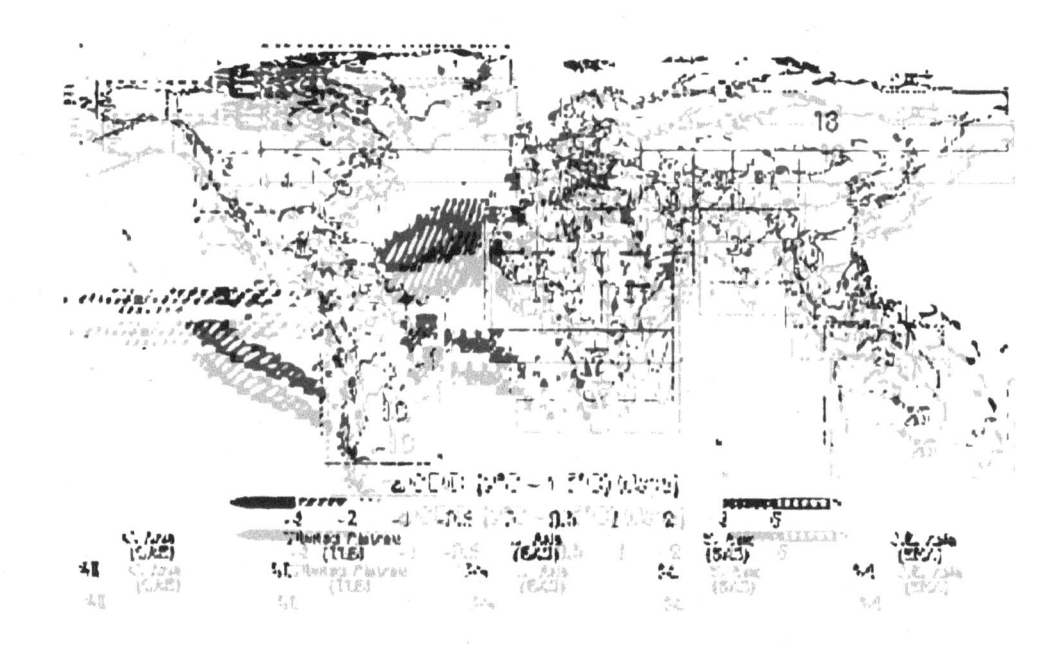

Elegy with Barbed Wire Swaddling a Fortunate Child, as Barbed Triptych Assemblage

Voices:

[Speaker1]
{Speaker2}
#Speaker3#

Staging Notes:

A single fencepost in the middle of the stage. From the fencepost, a single line of barbed wire spirals and clusters into a large mass immediately next to the fencepost. A center, upstage lamp on floor washes the stage and shadows into the audience. Offstage, an old oil barrel, half full of abandoned pots and pans, should be rolled back and forth for the entirety of the reading. Ideally, the barrel-roller should be a volunteer member of the audience.

[Tell me,]{what I cannot see,}#plain and curtain.#[How]#a knuckle opens to the bone, how#[my father's knuckle later blooms to bone.]{Boxcutter. Careless shipping and receiving. And I watch}#the doctor. Scrape the seam. My father#[says nothing.]{A fortunate child may}#or may not wince, or thrash.#[The wind creates constraint,]{ignores consent. There is}[no iodine for a fortunate child. There is dust. There is dust]{swallowing a wound.} [There is dust. There is dust gleaning wounds.]{There is dust thirsting wound.}#A wound is unwilling, until the body lapses.#{A fortunate child cannot scream. There is gurgling. There is dust.}#A brimming windpipe#[A fortunate child breathes in particulate toward a bronchial pile.]{A fortunate child does not see the sun.}#There is no sun.#{There is newspaper. Newspaper says for 12 minutes, nothing.}#There is no evidence#[of a fortunate child laying still on a Midwestern plain.]#My father's father left that plain to stop farming.#[He butchered]#in California.#[No evidence, all parceled.]{A fortunate child perceives light.}[It is not light.]#It is the sensation of razorstring peeling the body in 47 places at once#{on a newdesert altar.}[How a visiting priest once came to our church.]#I was a child.#{Told everyone his research.}[Sold everyone]#the true image of a christ post-scourging.#{More flesh than skin. Everyone bought the rendering.}[The frayed man was not smiling and still bound.]{A fortunate

16

child is bound}#to lay wrapped until exhumed.#[Sought only after a town attempts to account for bodies]{and the dust clears. An unfortunate child} [tumbles into a drift and drowns]{in arid.}#Returns the earth. A rescuer can only mystify#[how long a fortunate child can remain still]{and in agony. Ask}#a fortunate child#[what it is like to see nothing and feel everything wretch]{on the interior, split. My mother is relieved her child is}#low on melanin.#{A fortunate child who passes through}[rooms, conversations, interviews, traffic stops, local lending and loans.]#Do not forget in a fortunate child who has slept in emptiness.#{And refused to leave.}

The Nocturne Arrives, Temprano

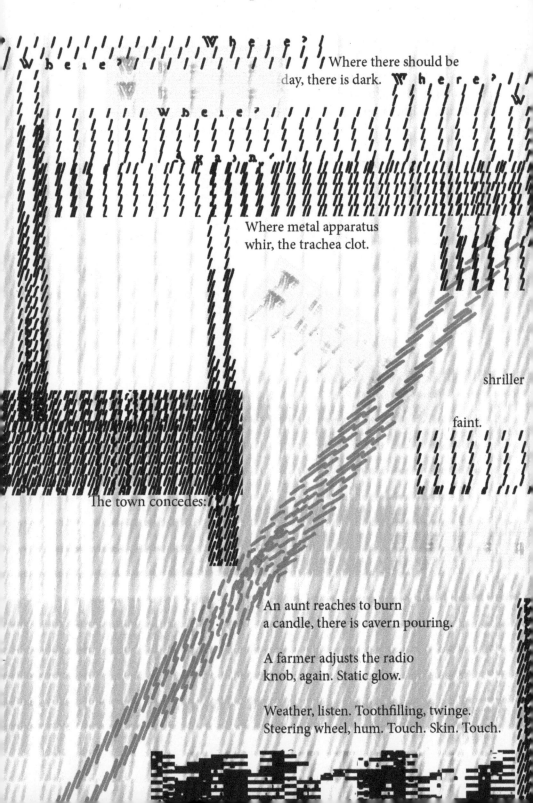

Where there should be
day, there is dark.

Where metal apparatus
whir, the trachea clot.

shriller

faint.

The town concedes:

An aunt reaches to burn
a candle, there is cavern pouring.

A farmer adjusts the radio
knob, again. Static glow.

Weather, listen. Toothfilling, twinge.
Steering wheel, hum. Touch. Skin. Touch.

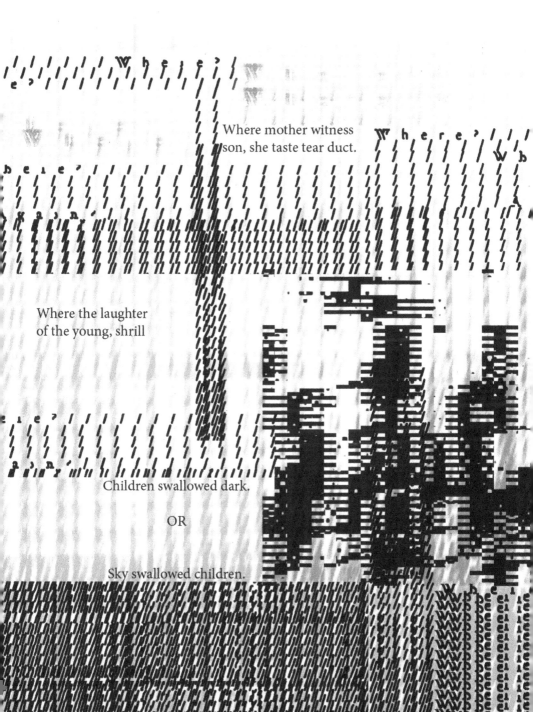

Where mother witness
son, she taste tear duct.

Where the laughter
of the young, shrill

Children swallowed dark.

OR

Sky swallowed children.

Crackling.
People.

Examination of Ruin

"you can see what they mean when they say '_leveled_' to the ground."

– Inscription on back of final photograph

AManUtters*RomeWasNotBuilt*

ExtinguishedEmpires.

InADay.True.AndNo

OneAsksHowManyMoonsPass

TheSameWayAlphaOmegaAre

Tomorrow'sSunrise?

ConsideredComplete

Circles.WhoThinksOfEndingIn

Perhaps The Remnants See Lens.

Roof. Staircase. Tree.

Documents Decay.

Notice How Each Thing Sloughs.

Undress The Lumber And Seed.

Your Land. It's Owned.

Call It Shanty & Shack

But Not Home. This Land Is Not

ABulldozerIsNotNature.Nor

GraspDismantling.

IsDisplacmentOfSelf

ButAJobPays.TheMaster'sTools

SomeonePosits *TheUntochedIs*

OthersHere.Here.Hear.

Mine.AllOfIt.Earth

Remains*ToSayIShared ThisWith*

On the Edge of a West Texas Family Farm, 1935

Assess the chickens.   Three. All hens.
         Windmill and roof.   Sturdy.
                        Tree.
                        Green.
                        Bushes.
                        Fibrous.
                        Fence. Intact.

Front and center is the cumulus above
the house. Messianic and obscuring
the sun, casting shadow and light. Postcard.
Prayer. A meditation toward the after. Share
this photo with 10 others and they will be saved,
or at the least understand the awe of god.
                   Except—   where there should be
                                crops, there is dirt.
                                Where there should be
                                cattle. There is crow.
                                Where there should be
                                family. Echo. Where
                                there should be farm.
                                There is wilt. There is
                                nothing. There is nothing
                                mystical in this photo. Inside,
                                a family packs. Or, prays
                                to the cloud asleep
                                over their home. Give us
                                rain. Give to us. There is
                                no god inside this house
                                or cloud to hear, at
                                sunrise the occupants
                                head west or east, just not here.
                                The cloud will have left
                                too. Sun-light will cook,
                                clean.

          Wind
          will scrape.   And gather.
          Earth will
          draft   primacy.

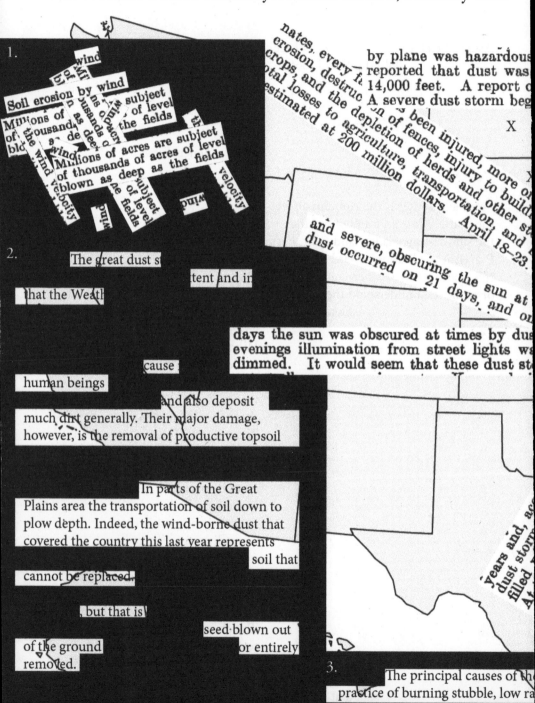

1.

Soil erosion by wind

Millions of

thousands

of

bld

the wind velocity

subject

of level

the fields

Millions of acres are subject

of thousands of acres of level

blown as deep as the fields

wind

velocity

wind

blown as deep

of level

the fields

nates, every
erosion, destruc
crops, and the depletion
tal losses to agriculture,
estimated at 200 million dollars.

by plane was hazardous
reported that dust was
14,000 feet. A report
A severe dust storm beg
been injured, more o
of fences, injury to build
of herds and other st
transportation, and
April 18–23.

X

and severe, obscuring the sun at
dust occurred on 21 days, and o

2.

The great dust s

tent and in

that the Weath

days the sun was obscured at times by dus
evenings illumination from street lights w
dimmed. It would seem that these dust st

cause

human beings

and also deposit
much dirt generally. Their major damage,
however, is the removal of productive topsoil

In parts of the Great
Plains area the transportation of soil down to
plow depth. Indeed, the wind-borne dust that
covered the country this last year represents
soil that
cannot be replaced.

, but that is

seed·blown out
or entirely
of the ground
removed.

3.

The principal causes of th
practice of burning stubble, low ra

years and,
dust stor
filled
At

control

ifficult. Several aviators
ntered at all levels up to
storm of April 22 follows:
1 a. m. and continued all

By the morning dense dust clouds covered the sky and this

places uncovered newly sown grains.

The dust storm affected this vicinity

A veil of dust appeared in the air

'0th
of the coloration of a sprinkling rain which occurred at that ti
condition ntinued all day.

the State indicate that this storm was pro

soil
of
e

severe of its kind ever experienced. Much seed was un-

First evidence of the Western dust

X

in the
erially
a kind

covered or blown out, especially on light soils, where in

the brightness of the sun was much reduced

e opinio
ur in Iowa.

extreme cases as much as 90 percent was reported lost.

X

X

but with debris of variou

The air was d

many, the

could not be distinguished at

X

50 feet. This gale caused loss

destruction of property. Dust

oly the most

Sun set yellow due to dust.

rous   intensive cultivation, the
and lack of organic matter to hold the soil in place. The loam and light s

blow

the field

Calculating the Load of Wind at the Weather Bureau Station

identify area in which wind persists

accept current
pressure of airstream

a dimensionless quantity
used to calculate the drag
or resistance of an object
in a fluid environment

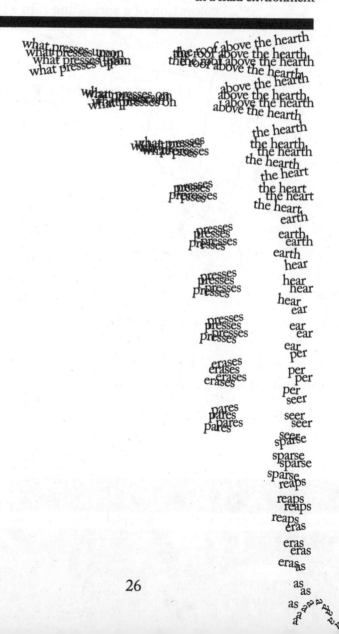

what presses upon
what presses upon
what presses upon
what presses upon

the roof above the hearth
the roof above the hearth
the roof above the hearth
above the hearth

what presses on
what presses on
above the hearth
above the hearth
above the hearth

the hearth
the hearth
the hearth
the hearth

what presses
what presses

the heart
the heart
the heart

presses
presses

earth

presses
presses

earth
earth
earth

presses
presses

hear
hear
hear
hear

presses
presses

ear
ear
ear

erases
erases
erases

per
per
per
per

pares
pares
pares

seer
seer
seer

sparse
sparse
sparse

reaps
reaps
reaps

eras
eras
eras
eras

as
as
as
as
a

It was conditions of this sort which forced many farmers
to abandon the area, Spring '35, New Mexico

Vestiges migrate.

Officials visit   every   barn,
                                            building,
                                            and outhouse,
inventory
the abdication:

— the umbra of cow [73]
— the umbra of chair [696]
— the umbra of herd of goats [12]
— the umbra of fetus [5]
— the umbra of family of 4 [9]
— the umbra of butterfly [483]
— the umbra of family of 6 [18]
— the umbra of family of unknown number [235]
— the umbra of snapped, and gnawed, femur [2]
— the umbra of man, sitting on chair, hands covering face [28]
— the umbra of shoeless child, rubbing eyes [32]
— the umbra of man, walking on side road heading out of town [939]
— the umbra of coughing mother applying mask to niece [638]
— the umbra of man, walking on side road heading into town [16]
— the umbra of child, holding headless doll [74]
— the umbra of unrealized corn field [24,433]
— the umbra of over-realized corn field [1,049]
— the umbra of unidentifiable migratory birds, unperched [144,023]
— the umbra of aunt writing family, *is there room* [3]
— the umbra of fly, shriveled, on cup and waiting [830,393]

— the umbra of sign that reads, *if you can read this, we are gone* [4]

The Basilica of Dust

No living
form

The Basilica of Dust
before the sun, barks at the light,
pours its own foundation

The Basilica of Dust settles
but does not open doors.

There are no saints in The Basilica of Dust,
There are no icons in The Basilica of Dust,
There are no psalms in The Basilica of Dust,
There are no candles in The Basilica of Dust,

The Basilica of Dust proselytizes cough.

The Basilica of Dust invites itself in -
a door,
a keyhole,
an unsealed window,
an unmasked

The Basilica of Dust asks no recitation of prayer,

and is giving you sacrifice.

Here,
every breath

The Basilica of Dust.

stands

over the built
over
the transfigured.

there are no miracles.
there are no eyes.
there is no tongue.
there is no air.

a crack,

inhale.

The Basilica

of Dust is

in you,

corrals.

2815-E.
Photo by Lange.
mills N. Mexico. Corral buried in
drifted dust. 1935
2390

29

After Russian Thistle, Leave

A mother gathers the dryness and walks across the vacant and brines.

Thinking of the angle of fence post, the lean is not with the wind, the matter shaping the corners into a late evening haze.

Thinking of the iridescent barbed wire as breathing.

A mother carries everything to the table and jars and jars and jars and jars and jars and jars until winter.

Exiting a season is a method into antlering abandonment.

Exiting a parcel is the attrition in which a household realizes disintegration is not linear.

A mother is a pantry, and a pantry is emptied until it is filled with dust.

Seeing the horizon as infinite, a road that leads toward sunset has no end.

Seeing the neighbor walk into the sun means that there is an instance where a shadow is consumed.

A mother asks the eldest to open two containers onto the cast iron and flame.

Counting the ribs on each of the living cattle is not a painting, or a pastime, but the encumbrance of distended children.

Counting the prologue, when a family packs their belongings, there are three acts; the third is a smeltcloud consuming both real and imaginary.

A mother distributes what is warm and pickled onto each of the plates unequally, everyone eats and looks out the obscured window, no one speaks because no one believes that what they see outside is a cloud, no one believes.

Effacing an empty house creaks, until square becomes parallelogram becomes heap

Effacing an upturned soil is the wind, headed in the direction of elsewhere.

To wake a coercion of pangs.

Solitude; or, Along a California highway, a dust bowl refugee bound for Oregon

Others arrive. Water jug. Smoke. Boiling tin. Kindling. Caffiene as midday exhaustion. You compass the masked campsite. Perhaps you see your farm. Perhaps you imagine coastal redwood rains. Perhaps you shield your eyes to not see what is not there, a wife, whose watch you wear with a wedding band. She is earthed elsewhere. Unsaid ritual before leaving, name each tree on the horizon. All after her. Look, puddles.

This land is your land, Holtville, California

consider the stress of the speaker's words:

    – land   *– your*

– this   *– my*

                                         consider

consider

        the dust bowl refugees abandoned
        TiresPaintCansChickenWireBasinsGasCansWiringMetalsBitsPiece
                    after planing away

consider
when uttering   *this land was made*
                       for you and me

consider   anger along the bend   of a rusted
             sheet of metal   slowness upon
                           the barb of a wire

and the ancestor
of the here   before
and the
offspring   of the seasons
                              yet

consider

the carbon footprint   of dust of you of me of paint can
after you me   are piled on ingested and sluiced

of the unsold harvest
     for you   for me

... this land is my land

the omission of the lyrics: Was a high wall there that tried to stop me
A sign was painted said: Private Property,
But on the back side it didn't say nothing

the plains

the leaving

above

consider
can
remains
a quiet
yield

"Stop. Go put you shoes back on. They'll know we Okies.", a Lost Image Reclamation

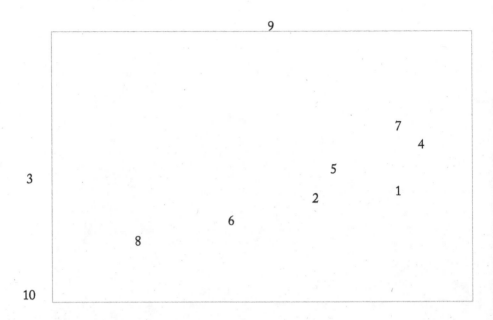

1. You sit
   on Grandpa's lap.
2. Mom & Grandma
   are next to you.
3. Dad attempts
   to set the timer.
4. Grandpa, the only fragrance
   you remember, smells
   of a stagecoach,
   glass bottle of aftershave.
5. Grandma is permed.
6. Mom clutches her purse.
7. You laugh at Grandpa
   popping out his dentures.
8. Before Dad sits,
   Grandma catches you
   barefoot.
9. You hear nothing in a photograph.
10. You lace; & Grandma begins
    dusting, a jackrabbit cries
    numerator, knowing.

A Dust Bowl Field Recording, Arvin, CA, 1940

i.

[RE]Live

the quell of breath
and [RE]sound
dust spilling

in. [Pause] A recording   captures
the wind skip skip skip skip skipskip skipskip skip skip skip skip skip

A BOY

skipping
into the night- [inaudible] [inaudible] mare

of a boy.   He is not
asleep.   He is frozen,
staring   into sky.

BLURTS

BLURTS

ii.

The catacombquiet   is inside

    the billows   mouthing

                                     eviction

street signs   a teeter-totter

                children.

A BOY

35

iii.

Study the voice of dreams in a dim snow.

Repeat
the aforementioned
twice. Observe   etched traceries hesitate.
                                                       Elevate the volume 15%,

replay.

A BOY The ethnographers' *BLURTS*

question remains muffling the speaker.

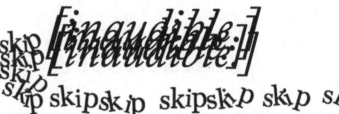

skipskip skipskip skip skip

Play the track,
two times slow. The layer of [PAUSE] is an unpaid
echo in the mechanics of site, an elder gustmemory of afternoon.

iv.

The clouds were never meant   to   metabolize
                                     hurt.

vii.

"It lasted for 15 hours."

vii.

To stifle sky

tape the seam of a window,
tape the seam of a window,
tape the seam of a window,
tape the seam of a window,
tape the seam of a window,

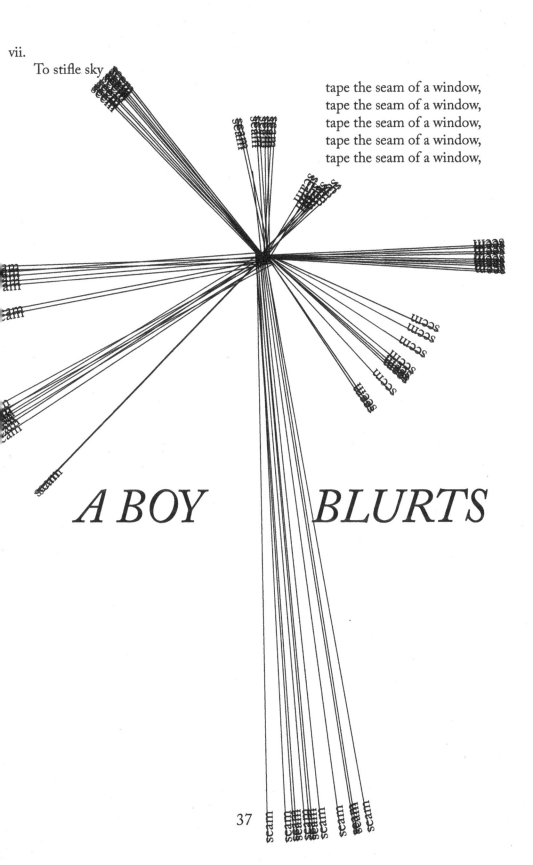

A BOY   *BLURTS*

Nothing but a Margin, but a Yield; Assembly Ritual

1. Walk outside.
2. Whisper / into the nearest tree / *Will I be here tomorrow?*
3. Answer your own / question / and look directly into what remains / of sun.
4. Return.
5. Consider the 3 feet {cough} by 9 feet landscape {cough} the dust bowl {cough} ballads of Guthrie {cough} the UN Climate Report {cough} tilling {cough} / the sun.

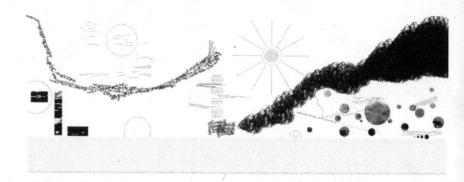

6. {cough}
7. {cough}
8. The landscape is broken.
9. {cough}
10. We have broken the landscape.
11. Detach all 64 / artifacts from the spine.
12. Sun Ra remains seeing, space is the place.
13. Locate what Sun Ra speaks of.
14. Assemble 4 rows: Numbers 1-15, then below, 16-31, then below 32-47, and then below, 48-64.
15. Await nature.
16. Perhaps another / will gather what we did not / affix.

Nothing but a Margin, but a Yield

To assemble "Nothing but a Margin, but a Yield" as a double-sided deck with disassembled muralpoem and annihilation strategies visit and print out the pdf via the QR Code below and utilize the previous poem "Nothing but a Margin, but a Yield; Assembly Ritual", to assemble the poem:

To project "Nothing but a Margin, but a Yield" as a 9' x 27' muralpoem onto a wall, acquire a projector, download the image via the QR Code below, and project the poem on the wall of your choosing:

41

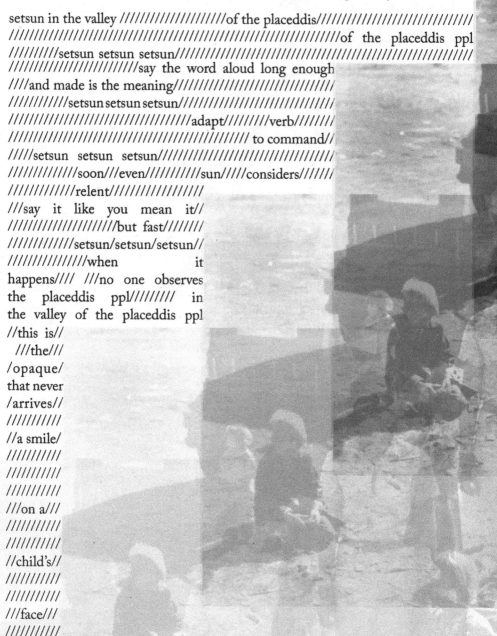

Everywhere I Sleep, I see Dust Bowl, 1.0

with Dorothea Lange's photo "Oklahoma mother of five children, now picking cotton in California, near Fresno." (1936)

"Allow us to explain ourselves. In the beginning we were dusty, we were lovely, we were turned around."

- from "Immigrants" by Farid Matuk

setsun in the valley ///////////////////of the placeddis//////////////////////////////
///of the placeddis ppl
//////////setsun setsun setsun///
////////////////////////say the word aloud long enough
////and made is the meaning///////////////////////////////
//////////setsun setsun setsun///////////////////////////////
//////////////////////////////////adapt/////////verb////////
/// to command//
/////setsun setsun setsun///////////////////////////////////
//////////////soon///even//////////sun/////considers///////
////////////relent//////////////////

///say it like you mean it//
////////////////////////but fast////////
//////////////setsun/setsun/setsun//
////////////////when   it
happens//// ///no one observes
the placeddis ppl////////// in
the valley of the placeddis ppl
//this is//
   ///the///
/opaque/
that never
/arrives//
///////////
//a smile/
///////////
///////////
///////////
///on a///
///////////
///////////
//child's//
///////////
///////////
///face///
///////////

/////
/////
/////
/////
/////
/////
/////
//////the   eyes///////////////
///////of a family///////////////
///////averted////////////////////
////in   the   statedream///
/////she gathers corneas///////
////////////////////////////////
//along the embankment of//
/////////////////////////////
//////////////////////////highway180/////////////////
//////setsun   setsun   setsun////
////until silhouette stands on a porch//////
///
///////////arm extended//////toward me//////////
///
/////////this   is   harvest///////////////
///////////////////////shesays////////////////////////////
///////////////i am distracted by the rooster////////////////////
/////////////////who abandons the solar for landgrief//////////////////////

43

Everywhere I sleep, I see Dust Bowl, 2.0

with Dorothea Lange's photo "Between Tulare and Fresno on U.S. 99. Highway gas tanks and signboard approaching town. See general caption." (1939)

somewhere in the bible it says give to caesar what is caesar's. and i know in the removal. in the signage along a sleeping highway and tankers a tie. i don't own a tie. i don't know how to tie a tie. when i tie a query sheet in which i list nothing and know so little in finance to say no. i know no matter tongue i will not answer him in the affirmative

the man eventually stops talking and moves his head. his head tells me the answer is

vhat that means. i'm catholic. and in the empire, ownership is in the taking.
)f gasoline. in the dream, i walk into the bank and ask for a loan to buy a house. i wear
l tie i search the internet. this is how the man asks me of my assets.
hat the man begins speaking in a dead language. all i know is how
vaking or sleeping. the subconcious knows. this is not my road.

negative. in my dreams i know i cannot ask. awake, i ask the internet the # of banks

and the internet provides
an answer: 4,600 branches.
an expansion of 931.17%
since 1939. i am unable
to apportion bank ownership
beyond 100%. to own
permanence. a perpetual
construct i cannot fashion
a pie chart depicting 1,000%.
1,000%? this is the effort
my grandfather exerted
to remember his grandkids
names. how he ran through
real and invented.
names like the soil, unfamiliar
in the mouth, until swallowed
by a dust storm at lunch.
a sudden ownership
of the light beyond a harvest.

Everywhere I sleep, I see Dust Bowl, 3.0

In the new America, stand upon the dead. In the new America, posture on the fall

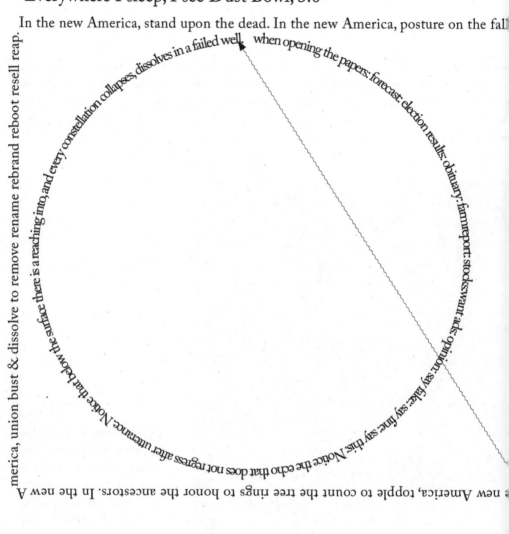

when opening the papers: forecast: election results: obituary: farm report stocks want ads: opinion. say fake: say fine: say this: Notice the echo that does not regress after utterance. Notice that below the surface there is a reaching into, and every constellation collapses, dissolves in a failed well.

merica, union bust & dissolve to remove rename rebrand reboot resell reap.

new America, topple to count the tree rings to honor the ancestors. In the new A

A
y ㄥㄣ t
man   can
say   nothing   &
lean   into   the   yoke   of
others, never   learn   the   names
of the animals or name of the crop
& the price. At market, not then or now,
but inside the onion, sits an unraveling that is not
passive, but kinetic. If learned soon no one plants the
bulb, no one stays to see the stalk, no one. A yt man knows
the logic studied & processed it, built a frame for the purchase,
turns the soil, the almanacs, the daylight, says rain. In a book, the data is
gathered, graphed, & indicates that February was coldest & precipitation was
absent, for the moment a yt man says try to project your thoughts as positive & smile.

lay Noah, print two. In the New America, pitch a tent, sleep, and call it your land.

America, document atrocity, and sell documentation. In the new America, p

n the new America, parasite the ancient. In the new America, fell & sell. In the new

Everywhere I sleep, I see Dust Bowl, 4.0

with interview about dust storms, sleet storms, and tall stories (part 2 of 2)
from Library of Congress Archive interview with Charlie Spurlock
Arvin, CA, FSA Camp, July 28, 1940

1) You listen to the voice of Charlie Spurlock.

2) You assemble a voicesculpture from the voice on the recording.

3) You download a transcription app on your phone.

4) You use the app to transcribe the voicesculpture.

5) You log the failed transcriptions:

> *Hey cardiac hill what are you all ready to storm out of the west over don't want to battle the way to another breeze on the web damn*

> *Where are you bled how are you I am on my way oil*

> *I am no I am I am on my way oil I am*

> *No no no red storm we are on our way no no no red storm*

> *No no no dust storm we are on our way No no no dust*

> *I am on my way now no no when I'm on my damage I'm on the way home I am*

> *Honey I'm on my way home damage west*

> *I'm on my way dust I'm on my way storm home I'm on my way*

6) You notice the repetition of *No* and *I'm on my way*

How even in the field recording of a man re-telling the story of a duster swallowing home, roof, windows, the sun, in a California migrant camp amid children crying and coughing and anthropologists prodding and listening a transcription app is wanting to make sense of all the *No* and *I'm on my way* jagged and uneven, carrying and optimistic. The crops have blown. The machines have scraped home. It is not here, the storm is, and *Where are you bled? I am.*

Everywhere I sleep, I see Dust Bowl, 5.0

with Dorothea Lange's photograph "Migrants' tents are a common sight along the right of way of the Southern Pacific. Near Fresno, California." (February 1939)

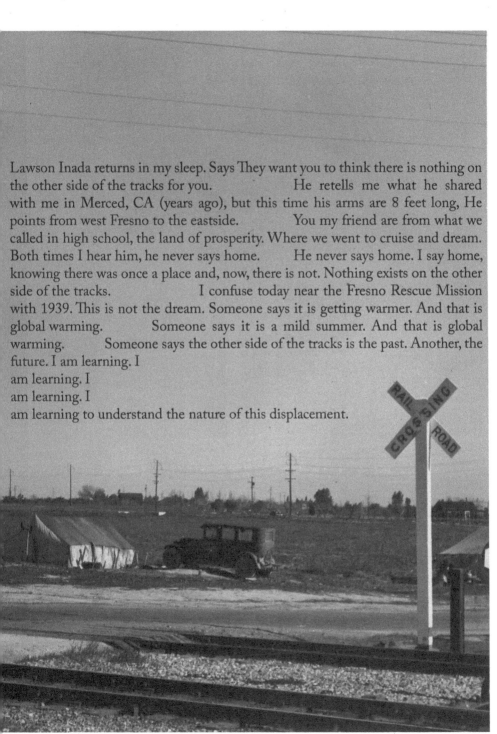

Lawson Inada returns in my sleep. Says They want you to think there is nothing on the other side of the tracks for you.   He retells me what he shared with me in Merced, CA (years ago), but this time his arms are 8 feet long, He points from west Fresno to the eastside.   You my friend are from what we called in high school, the land of prosperity. Where we went to cruise and dream. Both times I hear him, he never says home.   He never says home. I say home, knowing there was once a place and, now, there is not. Nothing exists on the other side of the tracks.   I confuse today near the Fresno Rescue Mission with 1939. This is not the dream. Someone says it is getting warmer. And that is global warming.   Someone says it is a mild summer. And that is global warming.   Someone says the other side of the tracks is the past. Another, the future. I am learning. I
am learning. I
am learning. I
am learning to understand the nature of this displacement.

Everywhere I sleep, I see Dust Bowl, 6.0

with Dorothea Lange's photograph "Highway City, California, near Fresno. See general caption. Family from Oklahoma; have been in California for six years, have been migratory workers now on Works Progress Administration from which they may be cut off at the opening of the 1939 harvest..." (May 1939), includes notes on back of photo, which read, "For cooking $5.00 per month approximately. They own a 1929 Ford. 'The cheapest thing for the government to do would be to put people like me on enough land to make a living on.' 'You can't tell me anything about running around with the fruit, I know that deal...'"

i   can   hear: good

how easy it is to make the

never asking who was

maybe it becomes an easy

how people want to build

who is really

not harvest as

the insatiable thirst

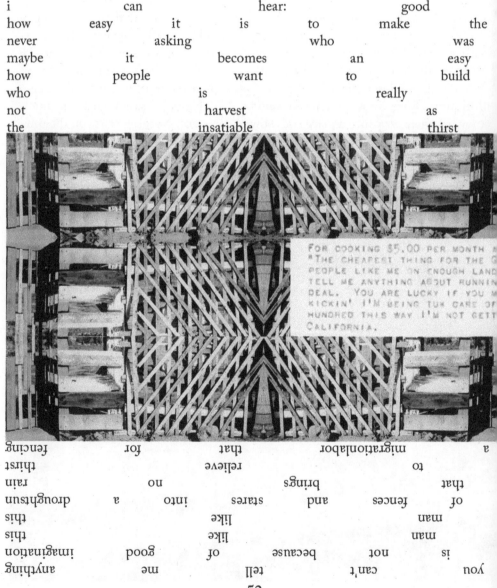

a migrationlabor that for fencing

to relieve thirst

that brings no rain

of fences and stares into a droughtsun

man like this

man like this

is not because of good imagination

you can't tell me anything

nces,   make   good   neighbors

sk   for   land   to   make   a   living

     on   it   before   arrival

assertion   from   behind   a   fence

a   wall   with   manufactured   fear

     getting   ahead   nowadays

          it   is   cannibal

          for   an   other

ELY.   THEY OWN A 1929 FORD.
  TO DO WOULD BE TO PUT
A LIVING ON."   "YOU CAN'T
WITH THE FRUIT, I KNOW THAT
ON TO GET HOME."   "I'M NOT A
I SHOULD LIVE TO BE A
NOWAYS."   MAY 1939

just   boundary   just   removal   just

     here   government   no
     here

decade   a   into   well

power   the   in   this   believes   like   man   a

     a   know   i

     you   know   a

appears   he   which   by   ease   the   and

says   who   man   a   imagine

Everywhere I sleep, I see Dust Bowl, 7.0

with Dorothea Lange's photograph "Between Tulare and Fresno on U.S. 99.
See general caption. Family inspect a house trailer with idea of purchase." (May 193

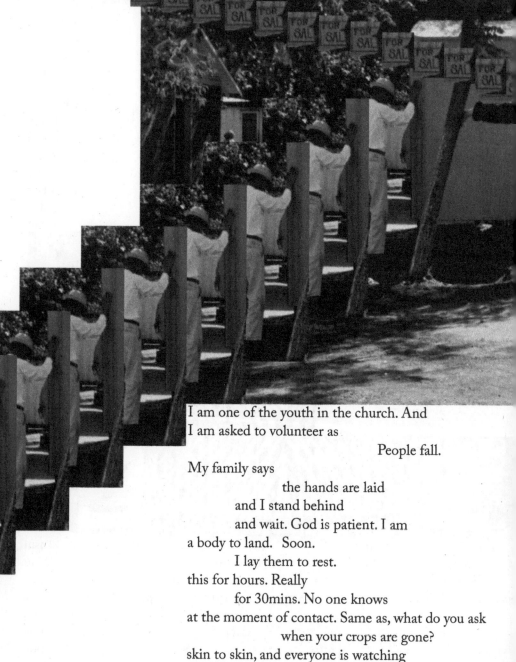

I am one of the youth in the church. And
I am asked to volunteer as

                          People fall.
My family says
          the hands are laid
      and I stand behind
      and wait. God is patient. I am
a body to land. Soon.
      I lay them to rest.
this for hours. Really
      for 30mins. No one knows
at the moment of contact. Same as, what do you ask
          when your crops are gone?
skin to skin, and everyone is watching
is patient.   A deal struck.

because I am tall and oversized,
     a catcher of the bodies.
     The priest says it is healing.
     it is the Holy Spirit.
     on the head

   patient and waiting,
       One falls. Then another.
Peaceful and at the base of the altar. I do

  what a priest says silently
      of a future home on wheels
       When all that heat applied
    that summer, This summer
      Someone falls.

Everywhere I sleep, I see Dust Bowl, 8.0

from Dorothea Lange's photograph "Irrigation pump on edge of field. Electric power typical of San Joaquin Valley farming. California." (February 1939)

the binary dies

with the climate.

no one
accepts

floods or deserts.

no one wants this to be the final answer. they want.
they want more.

over a loudspeaker the internet says   floods or deserts.

over the same loudspeaker a beached whale is trilling and grinding.

people demand: lower the volume.
the loudspeaker floods and becomes garbled.
the loudspeaker dries out and cracks.

everyone goes on the submerged loudspeaker to tell everyone else:
they don't want floods or deserts.

everyone is talking.
everyone.

in the ocean that swallows the mountains
all the grizzly scale the cliffs.
in the desert a buffalo catches cactus after cactus
until the hooving decodes
the whale's voice.

the ears puddle.

the hide of a buffalo is sold for the long winter.

Everywhere I sleep, I see Dust Bowl, 9.0

with Dorothea Lange's photograph "On the plains west of Fresno, California. Family of seven from Oregon dairy ranch which they lost. "We tried to get too big, I guess. Milk cans are all that's left of the dairy. Now pick bolls to make fifty cents to one dollar a day." (1939)

When I look away to recall the children, their hands are always linked. The grass
is a luminous green and I mistake the basin for a puppy sometimes, a cow
at others. A strong roof. Toys for all. The milk jugs are all full. No graves.
There exists a well that never thirsts. I am the punctum of revision.
Though fact-checking what I believe to see is easily accessible,
I refuse to lower my gaze to confirm. It is a b&w photo,
pristine and vibrant. A mother is calling them
in for a snack, for dinner before the elders
return from their labor. There is food
to eat. This is a home, not
a failing state. In the new
economy, climate
is good. Look
at all that
sun.

Everywhere I sleep, I see Dust Bowl, 10.0

from Dorothea Lange's photograph "Car trouble on west side of Highway No. 33 in San Joaquin Valley. Formerly a California cowhand and roving laborer. Now with his wife, he follows the fruit. 'My uncle homesteaded here sixty years ago. I'm lower on money than at any time.'" (1938)

The shape of a narrative is in the shadow of the conqueror. The conqueror's shadow omits the mirror.vShape a narrative without reflection.
            Hard: the voice
                        the edge
                            the culprit.

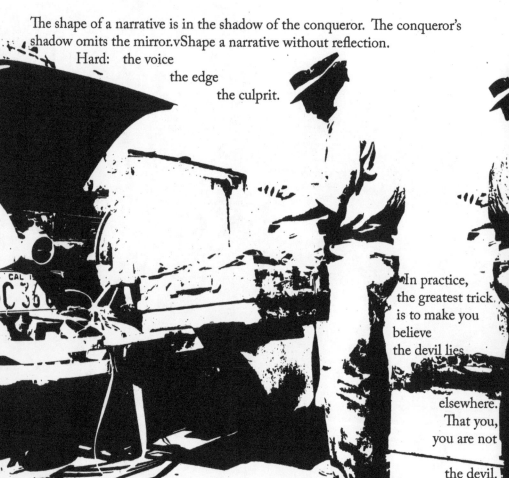

In practice,
the greatest trick
is to make you
believe
the devil lies

elsewhere.
That you,
you are not

the devil.

I don't begrudge the story, but I have a problem with the sinner.
How a southern yt man speaks against the homestead because he owns slaves,
A poet from Fresno talks of all my yt sins forgiven. And, I am
160 acres. I know people were there before this was constituional,
Drought.   Wind.
Narrative shape. Believe in a system. In the shade.
            Plant a flag. Earth has never failed,
left the living unfed,
earth.

A priest tried
to tell me once
that the greatest
trick of the devil
is to make you
believe
he does
not exist.
The pronoun
is likely right.

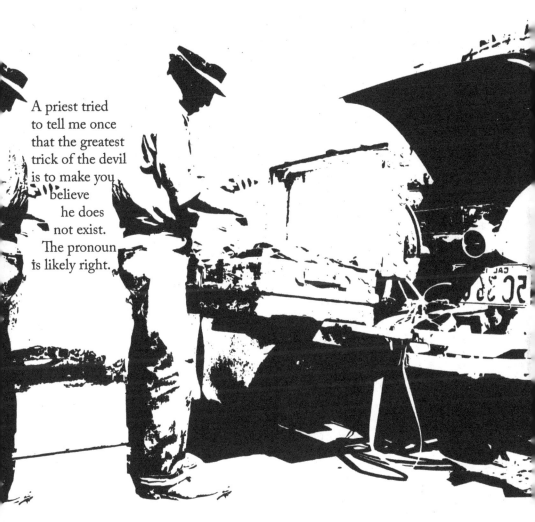

wants powervotescontrolwealthdominionthestatushisfatherpromisedhim.
unsure who greenlit absolution, those are far too many to gift tenderness.
before a person could take and till and upturn everything.
Dust.   Fluke.
What does the system believe? Strap all things to a car. Leave for the valley.
never
homes the ill, retains the dead. Nothing consumes
Earth does not know your name.

Everywhere I sleep, I see Dust Bowl, 11.0

with Dorothea Lange's photograph "Fresno. On U.S. 99. Storefront of San Joaquin Valley town. California." (May 1939)

The length a pupil

remains staring into the space

of revenant, the further

a mind spills.   Tents.

                                   Furniture.

                                   Gardening equipment.

                                   Glass. Trailers. Paint.

                                   Waterhose. Canteens.

                                   A spoon.

A duster spews from behind a jar of twine

          and begins gorging.   Wrecking.

                            All in the store is split and bled.

A tiny kingdom, unraveled.

Tomorrow, something is for sale.

Then the after – there is something for sale.

Everywhere I sleep, I see Dust Bowl, 12.0

with Dorothea Lange's photograph "U.S. 99 on ridge over Tehachapi Mountains. Heavy truck route between Los Angeles and San Joaquin Valley over which migrants travel back and forth. California." (May 1939)

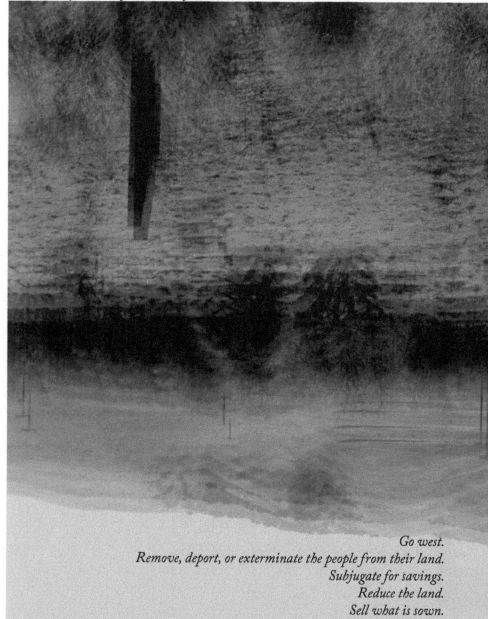

Go west.
Remove, deport, or exterminate the people from their land.
Subjugate for savings.
Reduce the land.
Sell what is sown.
These are the prices.
Pray for rain and harvest.
Put down the rails and roads for speed.
Put up telephone poles to communicate.
Put up fences to prevent animals and possessions from straying.

FENCE (N): EARLY 14c., ACTION OF DEFENDING, RESISTANCE; MEANS OF PROTECTION, FORTIFICATION, SHORTENING OF DEFENS.

We went west.
We removed, deported, and exterminated until it was our land.
We subjugated and profited.
We reduced the land and sowed.
We sold at market.
We accepted the prices.
We dreamt and the other labored.
We put in the rails and roads and wanted faster.
We erected poles and trenched cables and now phone in.
We put up fences and we never strayed.

Everywhere I sleep, I see Dust Bowl, 13.0

"If you owned a few of you could make me a visit."
    -Handwritten inscription on the front of a postcard of oil wells from Fresno County

imagine   pump   viscous   replace horizon   seeking   accessory

ocean   beneath   arrive   when disappears   results   output

sinking   crust   remember   return infinite   dreamaches   revenue

believe   all   green becomes derrick   transference   ventricle

false   matter turns   shallow after   breathing   crescents

apply   not   dry   waning derrick   crumbles   failure

become resurface   mistake   can machine each   commodity

"If <u>you</u> <u>owned</u> a <u>few</u> of <u>you</u> <u>could</u> <u>make</u> me a <u>visit</u>."

dinosaurs   things   postcard   happen   ask   construction   bottled

themselves   long   scratch   today living   return   sold

crude   dead   god's   go   give   different   money

memories   dreams   flailing   there until   liquid   made

asking   without   revision   stand death desired   claim

66

Everywhere I sleep, I see Dust Bowl, 14.0

"Ending a life of centuries, a giant tree falling, logging among the big trees, Converse Basin, California."

– description on back of image, a fallen tree

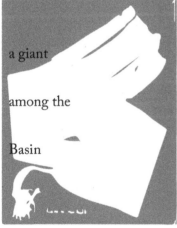

Ending
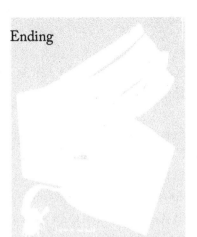

centuries,

logging

California.

Everywhere I sleep, I see Dust Bowl, 15.0

with Dorothea Lange's photograph "Employment signs in Spanish and English. Near Fresno, California." (1938)

The smartphone applications store provides a variety of navigational options for the consumer. Some free. Some not. But all options for the consumer.

A map to find take-out food. A map to bike. A map to run and track caloric burn. A map of flora trails. A map of fauna no longer living. A map of police presence in your neighborhood. A map of expansion. A map of acquifers beneath the surface. A map of weather projections. A map of elevations. A map of communities and peoples that have been displaced. A map of seized property. A map of imaginary creatures in the neighborhood. A map of where to find the cheapest gas prices. A map to avoid police d.u.i. checkpoints. A map to outlining dead tongues. A topographic map of graves. A map of irrigation. A map of oil through native lands. A map for sex. A map of sex. A map of ownership. A map of hate crimes and bus routes. A map of places in which you should see when visiting a city. A map of places you should never go when seeing a city. A map of peoples to avoid. A map to tell you all the places you want to go. And a map of all the places you have been but can never return to.

All the maps are downloaded, rated, ranked, updated, and discontinued.

The maps are translated into multiple languages.

The maps contain the information users input. The maps source users.

The userdata include's "Pursuit of Happiness" from Kid Cudi, and the track auto-plays on the smartphone. Wants to know, what I know about dreamin' (dreamin'). Only to tell me that I really know nothin' (nothing'). The repetition is acknowledging a call toward wakefulness. A call for the user to hear what another cannot offer. A call is a series of echoes that have managed to secure the understanding that an echo is not singular or isolated. The user understands that they are not alone and begins crying. Another user notices the emote, and asks what it means when a user emotes tears during a rap song. The user returns to the song. In this instance the two users begin understanding that they both are unsure what direction a new navigation application will provide either. The application is downloaded by both nonetheless, and they digress to the pursuit. A digression is a sense of orientation, a return to less than what has been accomplished along the path. In the new forward, the users seek and find the predetermined outcomes the algorithms selected as much desirable to the user. In the new forward, this is the happiness of a user navigating across a field and into the chrome of a carbonsetsun.

There is a cartographer in the desert. Not the desert known by the owner, but the desert known by the cartographer. The cartographer speaks in eons and sees the owner's effort to provide direction and is sad. The cartographer visits the owner, and the living cannot see they are in the cartographer's desert and thirst deeply. The owner does not recognize their thirst. The cartographer asks the owner why they have created a sign in which a translation is unequal. The owner scoffs. The cartographer is ignored.

A man on television will say that there has been progress. He, or his lineage, have owned the land, accumulated the wealth, profited from the bodies, and now have architectured a voice via the throatbox of bones.

This is the new economy and everyone can pull themselves up by their strapboots equally. The people watching the webcast do not own boots or strapboots.

He is shown a picture and asked to explain the equity of Spanish-speakers having to travel "⟵⟶■4 miles" while English-speakers only have to travel "⟵⟶■ 3 miles".

He studies the picture to frame his answer and, after 14 minutes, says the land is owned by the ranch and they are doing their part to care for their employees.

The man never blinks. And what is blinking. but an automatic recognition of perpetuity? The man is pleased in his pivot. He adds, if those people learn English they could understand the American Dream and take the shortcut.

There is no mention of cages or aerosols or borders or drought. Only carbon and crop yield. The yield is good. Yield is good.

The user listens to a streaming song and downloads the newest userdata targeted map application. Silence arrives via buffering. A collapse requires no bandwidth.

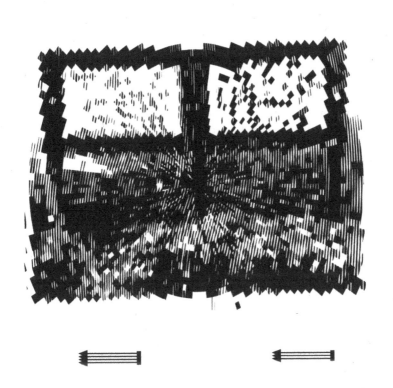

Untitled Searches, Postmetaphor

\<search\>
I am searching for a name not the dust bowl and I think about drought
and naming this a drought escapes the hand of man and escape
is such an easy word lightening loads and whatnot and man being
who he is responsible for so much it is easy to blanket from deere to
amherst to van buren to hoover to a lot of presidents thereafter
that a postmetaphor may underscore the departure of topsoil and/or breath

\<\<search\>\>
I am searching for a name not the dust bowl and I know there is a place
that my grandparents called home and I ask my mom not their daughter
of its name and she says sallisaw and if I tell you that named sounded
familiar it was because I read the grapes of wrath one time skipped
the dying pastoral chapters and decided instead to focus on the narrative
perhaps this is the precondition of being born in fresno and a poet
and that is also an escape tell a story no tell everything just leave
out the details in which I consider a dream in which I am only drinking
dust only the feeling all the feelings yes the feelings which I am drought

\<\<\<search\>\>\>
I am searching for a name not the dust bowl and I feel visiting the grave
of my grandparents will only provide a single piece of information their age
when they left home and clarity in the middle of a duster is in short
supply when all you have is your belt tied around your dog to help
lead you home and again this is postmetaphor as human is now reduced
or on equal footing with canines to decipher what is and where is
and perhaps equal footing oversells our contribution to the planet

\<\<\<\<search\>\>\>\>
I am searching for a name not the dust bowl and I discover a voice
of an audio recording a woman searching for her children the dust
does that sometimes etches what it wants into a mother's collarbone
and abandons all other evidence that it exists everything now
and at the hour of our death in the punctum of smoothness

<<<<<search>>>>>
I am searching for a name not the dust bowl and I ask myself
if I would have left or stayed am I not the spittle in the corner
of my grandfather's mouth dying of alzheimer's or the detached
hip socket of my widowed grandmother in a backyard since
bulldozed and flattened as if removing earth removes the memory
of earth knowing what earth has and always will be world without end

<<<<<<search>>>>>>
I am searching for a name not the dust bowl and I perceive an inability
to astrally project into the billow in 1935 and this is less of a bummer
because of the reality that I would be unable to breathe or observe
anything from within and again I am reminded this is all postmetaphor
and seeing nothing from the inside is a kind of clarity that statics
my organs in a way I find filling with dread filling with sand

<<<<<<<search>>>>>>>
I am searching for a name not the dust bowl and I dimensionally analyze
bowl as half sphere and wonder in the venn diagram of imagined gods
assessment there are ancestors of the dust bowl who also believe earth
is flat and now I am convinced that an algorithm will be coded
to present the data visually an app a 5-minute quiz a dongle that snaps
me into all the codecs I could possibly request I can virtually walk
through the data no even though I never learned to swim I will virtually
swim in data and learn of my DNA and the DNA of others and sort out
everything I have never wanted to know related to fear and dust and how
kismet descends upon a great plain plowed and plowed and plowed
and plowed and plowed until what is upturned ghosts

<<<<<<<<search>>>>>>>>
I am searching for a name not the dust bowl and I tell the mirror
I will invent a new word I will read the ancient texts glyphs rubble
rock I will read until my eyes dry my eyes bleed my eyes fall out and I fail
to recognize the limitation of my tongues

<<<<<<<<search>>>>>>>>>
I am searching for a name not the dust bowl and I bookmark 3 articles
on the heating of the oceans I resist reading them because I am sensing
a demise not how long it takes for a pot of water to boil but how long
a pot takes to stop boiling and the ocean is a big pot of water uninterested
in boiling all I see are orcas and otters and algae and coral and unknowns
arriving on shores belly up foul and we all will have a chance to jump in

<<<<<<<<<search>>>>>>>>>>
I am searching for a name not the dust bowl and I glitch nowhere
more near or away in the assemblage of anceintfuture destruction
and instead meditate upon the shape of my spinal column cleanly
detached from the self leaning forward in a post-hunchback posture
that can only escalate in the mausoleum of a latent memory that I ask
to leave but returns to me returns to me as the memory cache partitions

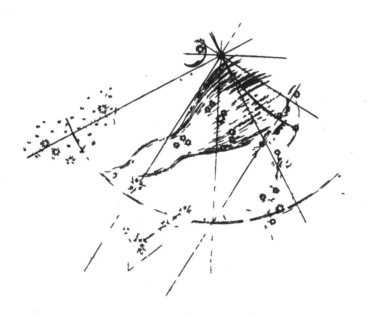

Analog Jaguar Digitalization Forest Canopy

after Francisco X. Alarcón and Juan Felipe Herrera

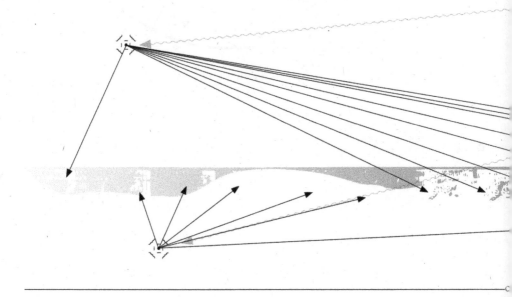

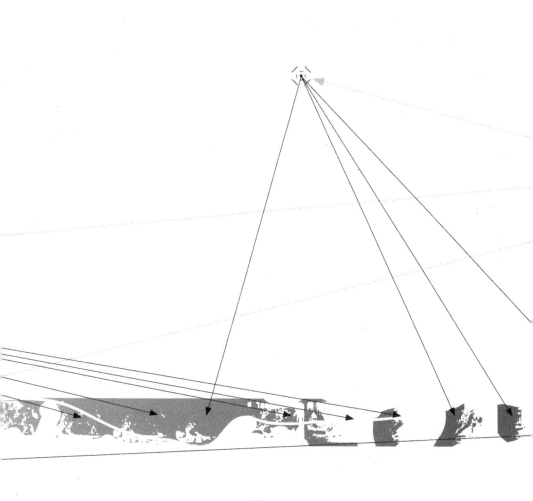

cage cage cage cage cage cage cage cage cage cage cage cage cage cage cage cage cage cage cage cage cage cage cage cage cage cage cage cage cage cage cage cage cage cage cage cage cage cage cage cage cage cage cage cage cage cage ca

stay   ancient   autonomous   scrub   datastreams

we   question   river   jay   assumes

the   stumbling   dammed   drinks   galaxy

animal   marrow   still   flits   jaguar

limb   synaptic   trickles   mimes   crumbles

A n a l o g J a g u a r D i g i t a l i z a t i o n F o r e s t C a n o p y

server   crossing   to   self   sky

algorithms echo   tree   inside   jaguar

what   steady   ring   last   earth

has   ascending   applied   remaining   jaguar

gone   relic   heart|palm   saguaro   particle

DustLore35

A man at a diner says, *Never read*
the newspaper, and continues to drink
his coffee and draw circles on want
ads. No one is walking out, every bird

in the state is regressing. They forgot
how to perch, slept in fields, blocked
the roads so The Leavers could not
leave for fear of flattening. They forget

feathers and abandon flight midsky,
plummet. The sound of a chest
cavity crumbling can be confused
with the explosion of a dirt clod

until you witness liquification. No
one is walking out, the sky's in the middle
of descent. A man at a diner laughs,
says, *See, they'll prolly say it hasn't rained*

                                                 in months.

The Dessicant

When the soil is   gone
    where do the living   bury
                      the desiccated?
                First   grama-buffalo
                                    wire
                                    bluestem-bunch
                                    sand grass-sand sage

—thirst.

When the grass is   gone
    where do the living   consume
                    the nutrient?
                Nothing: to root.
                                  Blacktailed rabbits
                                  Grasshoppers
                                Snakes Mice
                                Gophers
                                Prairie dogs
                                & Locusts

—leave.

When the living is   gone
    where do the living   placenta

                    the memory?
            Inside
            a raindrop?   A wind?   A storm?   A plain?

         A sacrum
—remains.

In A Season

Say she is   hardpan   in   the fields
                 in the debt   of a mortgage
                          of her church   and no matter
                          — her headstone stands
unpoured.

Say she wrapped   muslin around the mouth of her   self
                                          children

                        prepared
                        prevented
                        projected   erasure.

                                  Say she said to me
                                              others
                                            anyone
          there has been   drought
                        disaster
                        death
                        disappointment
                        in SpringSummerFallWinter
and that does not mean forget.

Say she
was an overexposure of kinlight inside desert
                                    inside marrow
                                      inside macramé hung on a dining
                                      room wall, weighing at the nail
                                      as the dust heaps, sagging,
                                      sagging until the nail sighs
                                      and relents, leaving the shadow
                                      of what was once on the wall, still
                                      on the wall.

                        Say she
                     is a beam
                     on which tidal exerts all night, expecting
            a sunrise, and all that is found is stone.

Dispossessed

                                           Take the land

                          Take the *land*
          Take the land

          & escape

                                        _____

              & escape
                        is breath
                              is breathing

                        is the clarity of looking out
                                   is leaving home to ask the air

                                        _____

                                        _____

Take the land

Take *the* land

———————————————

& seeing sky

———————————————

ask the air
if it understands
cleanliness
& if being
that close
to heaven
it forgets
the voice
of the living
& the earth

                                  & the earth is no less

    just not there,

               it is elsewhere,

                            or if they still wheeze
                            in & out

             where,

fence,

only dissolve
the lease & maintain

the pulmonary crop
ancestors plowed
as bank cannot capture
a rooted respiratory of acreage

than before,

        everything is here
        or there,

    elsewhere is what is said when it is not
    known where the people shelter

in the same way   as anew,
else-

                                  there is no

                no firmament,

   only dissolve

& answer a child
who asks where is home
with all that is is within
this breath

only dissolve
the lease & maintain

Piso de Piedra

    There are things I want to do,
        That I know I cannot.

I have walked into my own dreams,
and made demands.   Everyone laughed. I did not
fly or wake or evaporate or burn.
I sat and listened to the laughter.
I am not surprised. I have tilled
a desert: made grain, made god,
made fruit. In the dream, I tell
a boy, the hourglass holds all
the land, and I cannot undo
what I dismantle. He stares
and doesn't laugh. Offers
his left palm that is split
open. He says the hole
takes what the hole
takes. Maybe I am
next. Maybe you
are. Or, maybe
we are already
on the other
side. How
a stone
floor

cracks to analog the stable.

In watching Tiny Tim's "The Ice Caps Are Melting" (1968), I understand

It is not in the prophecy
or pitch or performance. And it is not as much as in the understanding,
                    I get it.   *The ice caps*
are melting.
        Or rather, have been melting for years.

I did this. And by I, I mean, you. And by you, I mean us.   All of us.
                                      Above
                                    and below.

This is not a hallucination.
The plural I hopes. In the same way
hope obscures the bones of denial.
The same way a YouTube uploader
called "The Ice Caps are Melting"
performance art on February 9, 2012.

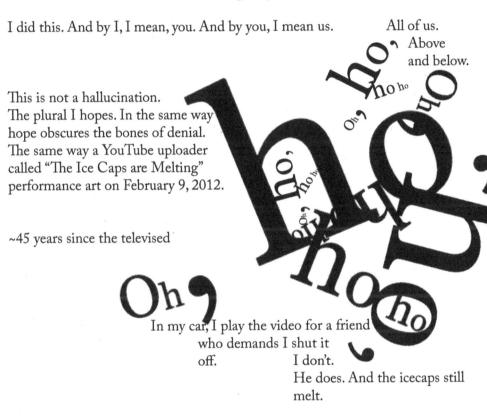

~45 years since the televised

        In my car, I play the video for a friend
           who demands I shut it
            off.   I don't.
                    He does. And the icecaps still
                    melt.

To find the same joy
in the chorus of children joining in song.

The same joy in the utterance of: drowning.
                                              sins.
                                              sea gulls.

The same joy in the earth knowing   the I
                                          will pass.

Megadrought, DustLore1.5°c

1. There is a line at 7/11 for MegaMillions.

2. There is a line for quickpicks all the way to the slurpees, and no line to fill out the ticket manually.

3. There is no pencil to fill in numbers with a lot of little lines.

4. There is a mega-sale for the business that are going out of itself, even furnishings and fixtures, that people snake a line through to buy.

5. They are closing because for a long time there was no lines.

6. There is a line at the bar that has been gentrified, it is also an arcade, and the young and mobile, who swipe and tap to avoid lines, play Megaman.

7. Megaman was imported from Japan, and before was called Rockman.

8. Rock does not sound mega-enough.

9. I only played Megaman for a while and got bored.

10. I was a child and got bored waiting in line with my mother at the welfare office, an office she helps now run.

11. My mother complains about the lines, not the people.

12. She buys MegaMillions hoping the numbers and stars align.

13. And even though I don't play lottery, I know that line grows the longer there are no winners.

14. I have a feeling the lines will only keep growing because MegaMillions sounds exciting.

15. I am already distracted from the idea of wealth, not climate.

16. Someone says to draw a line in the sand with climate change deniers.

17. The tides are higher and coming in, and Is this the point when Noah begins building?

18. I never ask myself questions, distracted by a mega-meal-deal board driving by a fast food chain, that has a line in the drive thru, think of the sharpness in pronouncing point in a 1.5°c increase.

19. In a line that moves incrementally, you suture the patience, how you adjust a thermostat that you adjusted a season too late.

20. I do the math and draw lines, reminding myself that MegaMillions is a numbers numbers game.

21. Walking with a friend, they tell me that a numbers game ran out of a liquor store doesn't make you rich, but it pays the rent.

22. I have been wondering if Earth should start charging rent.

23. The premise being Earth as owner, but how do you own the self?, who is the landlord?, and where do I send my security deposit?, are all the questions that come to mind.

23. Moreover, do I have to stand in line on the Prime Meridian to deliver my check?

24. Prime feels like another way to say mega, the mega-line.

25. The Prime Meridian is defined as a line of longitude at 0° and runs through Greenwich, England, its designation is arbitrary.

26. Arbitrary, how CalTrans decided to not buy up the side of the street of my family's house, creating a dead-end with poor lighting.

27. A dead-end with poor lighting is ideal for people to dump their garbage, burn stolen cars, rendezvous, and pile dead bodies.

28. When I say ideal, I mean an entire city has decided to line up to discard their sins 200 feet from where my mother and father still live.

28. More universal, an entire city can be shortened simply to an entire-ty, an entirety expelling waste near home.

29. What is the climate of Earth, if not the state of a home?

30. I hear climate and remember a 1.5°c increase through global warming means a megadrought in perpetuity.

94

31. Anything in perpetuity is exhausting.

32. A man in a lifted truck blasting Megadeth is next to me at a red light and peels out in a haze of smoke from the exhaust pipes when the light turns green.

33. Megadeth is meant to represent the annihilation of power.

34. The annihilation of anything is exhausting.

35. I would tell you the exhaust disappeared at the next light, but the truck was one of many in a long line of traffic.

36. I would tell you the exhaust disappeared when everyone left that intersection, but after arriving home I search a music database and discover that the most played song by Megadeth is "Symphony of Destruction" from the album "Countdown to Extinction".

37. A countdown is a line that asks you to meet its ed.

38. Years ago, I met an impeccably dressed, older Egyptian refugee, who volunteered at my first job after college and asked him about his suits and pronunciation of his last name.

39. The man says Americans pronounce it 'Mega-hed', and that is fine, I stand in line to get my benefits, but it is mispronounced, and the suits are the only things I took when I fled Egypt and my fortune seized by a new regime.

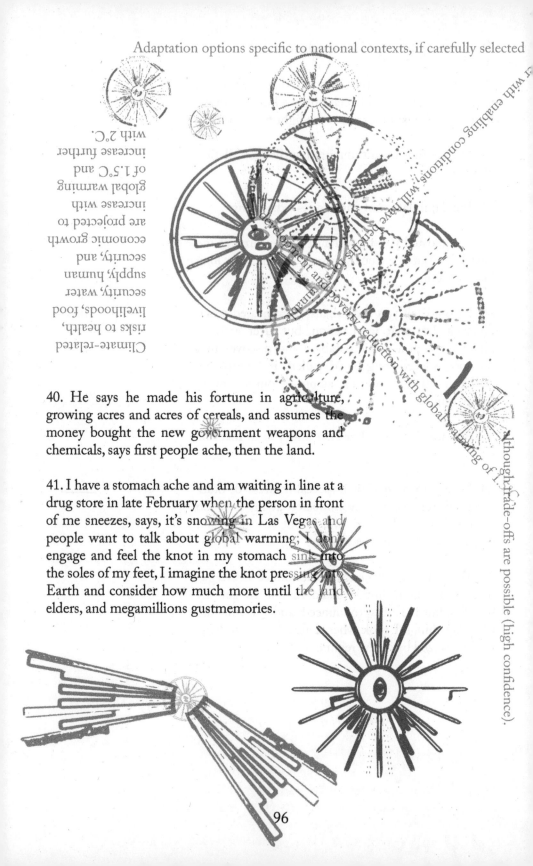

Climate-related risks to health, livelihoods, food security, water supply, human security, and economic growth are projected to increase with global warming of 1.5°C and increase further with 2°C.

...r with enabling conditions, will have benefits for ...development and poverty reduction with global warming of 1... Although trade-offs are possible (high confidence).

40. He says he made his fortune in agriculture, growing acres and acres of cereals, and assumes the money bought the new government weapons and chemicals, says first people ache, then the land.

41. I have a stomach ache and am waiting in line at a drug store in late February when the person in front of me sneezes, says, it's snowing in Las Vegas and people want to talk about global warming; I don't engage and feel the knot in my stomach sink into the soles of my feet, I imagine the knot pressing into Earth and consider how much more until the land, elders, and megamillions gustmemories.

a Neoapocalyptices

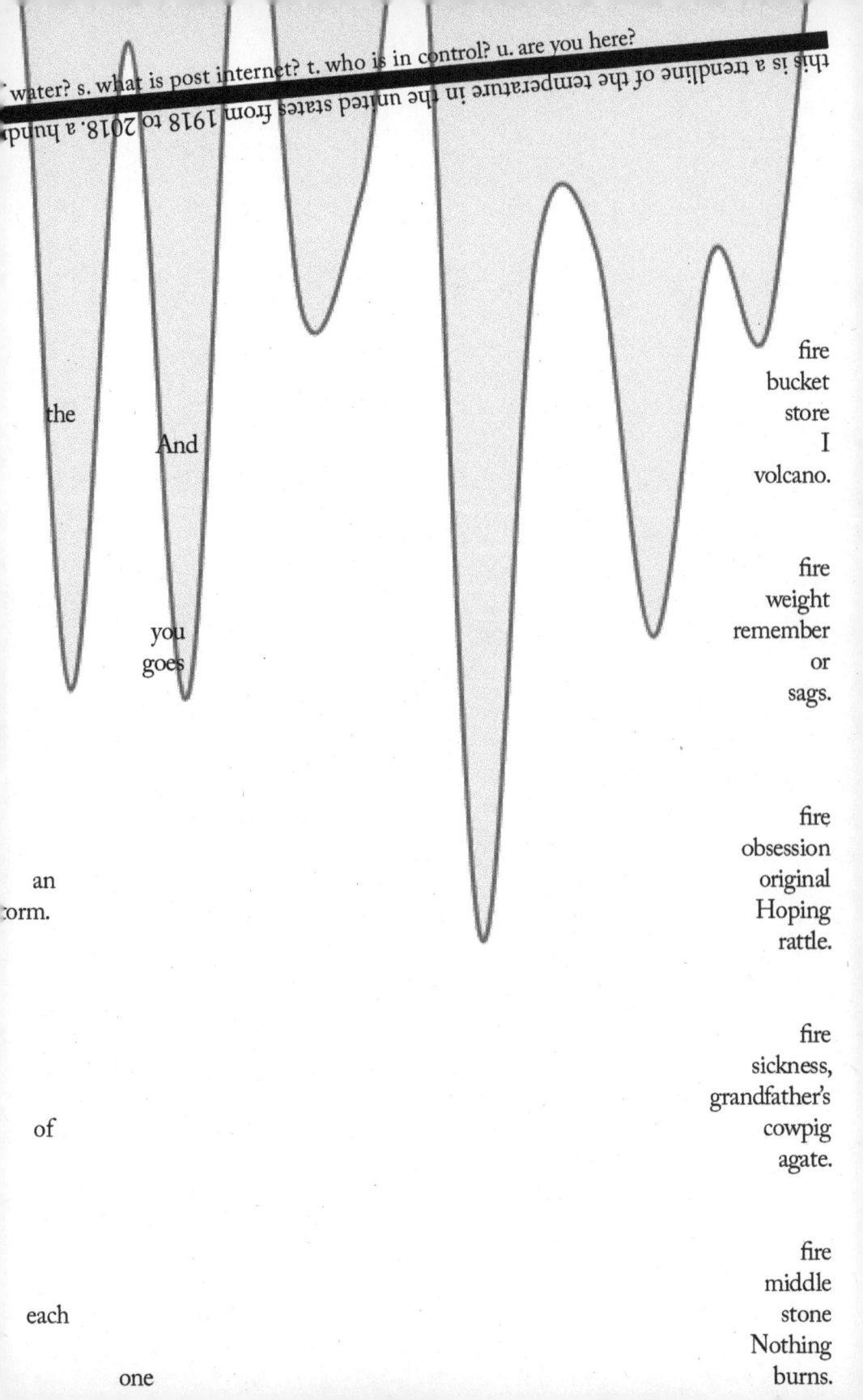

water? s. what is post internet? t. who is in control? u. are you here?

this is a trendline of the temperature in the united states from 1918 to 2018, a hund

the

And

you
goes

an
orm.

of

each

one

fire
bucket
store
I
volcano.

fire
weight
remember
or
sags.

fire
obsession
original
Hoping
rattle.

fire
sickness,
grandfather's
cowpig
agate.

fire
middle
stone
Nothing
burns.

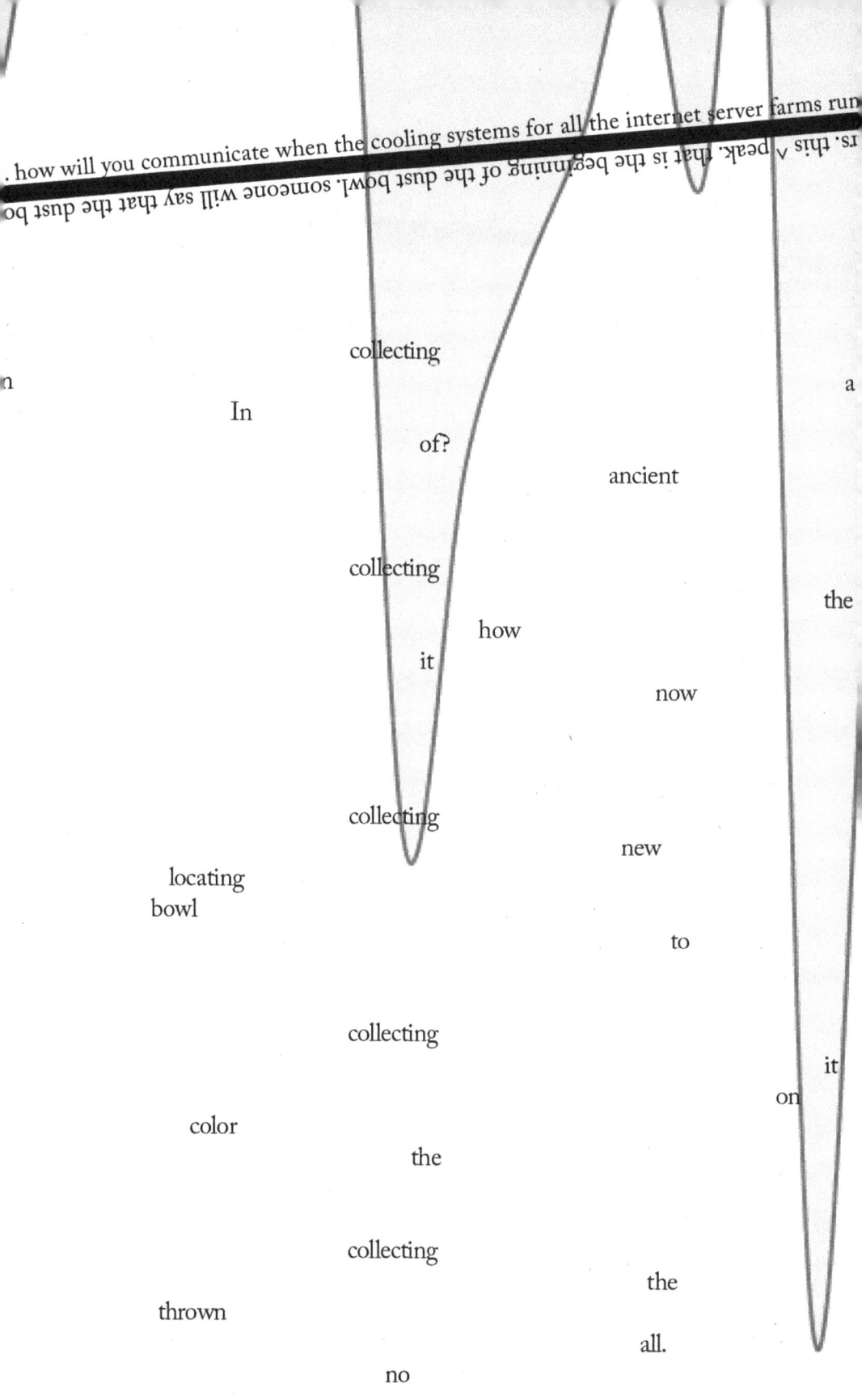

how will you communicate when the cooling systems for all the internet server farms run

rs. this A peak. that is the beginning of the dust bowl. someone will say that the dust bo

n

In

a

collecting

of?

ancient

collecting

the

how

it

now

collecting

new

locating
bowl

to

collecting

it

on

color

the

collecting

the

thrown

all.

no

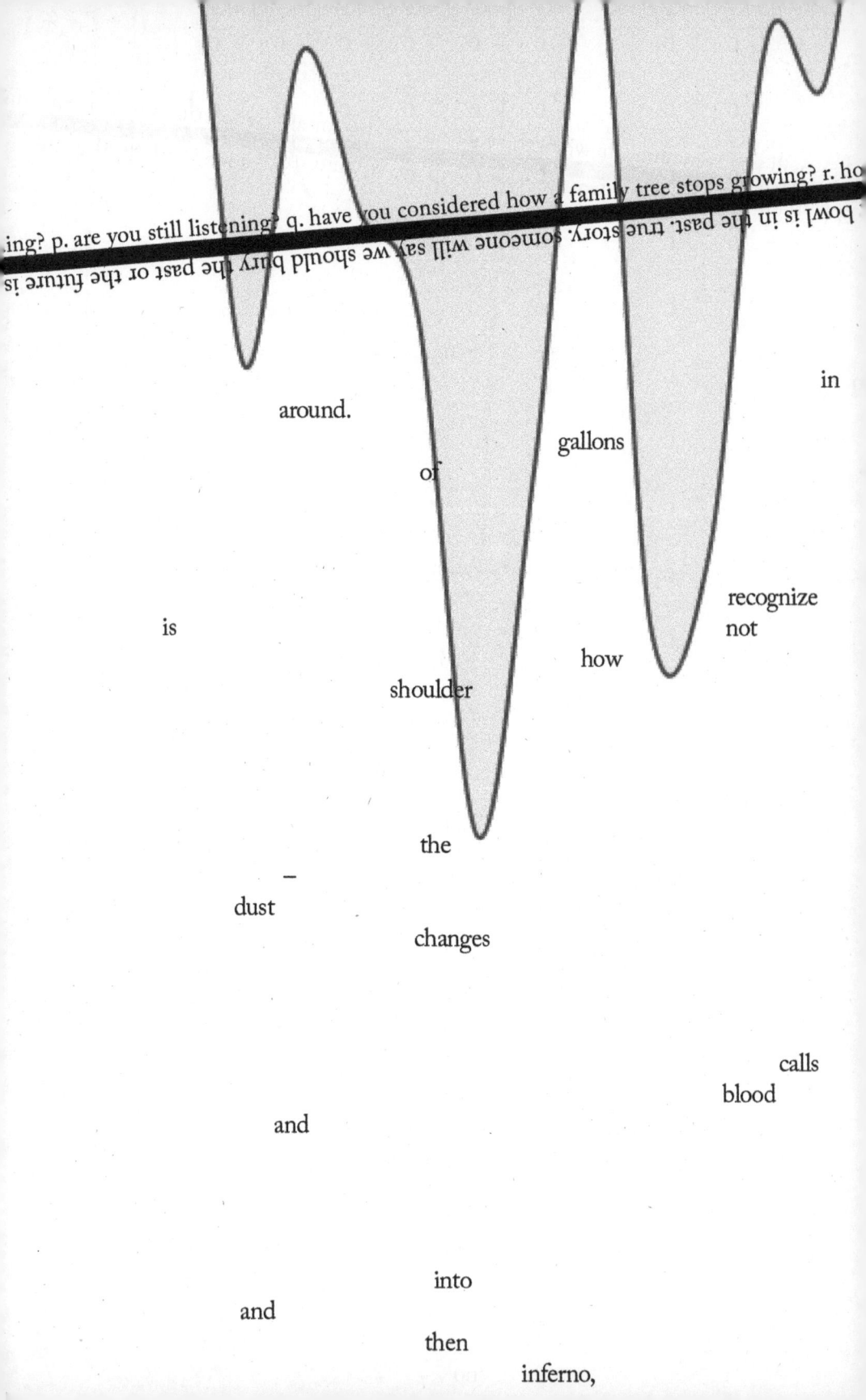

ing? p. are you still listening? q. have you considered how a family tree stops growing? r. ho

bowl is in the past. true story. someone will say we should bury the past or the future is

in

around.

gallons

of

is

recognize
not

how

shoulder

the

—

dust

changes

calls

blood

and

and

into

then

inferno,

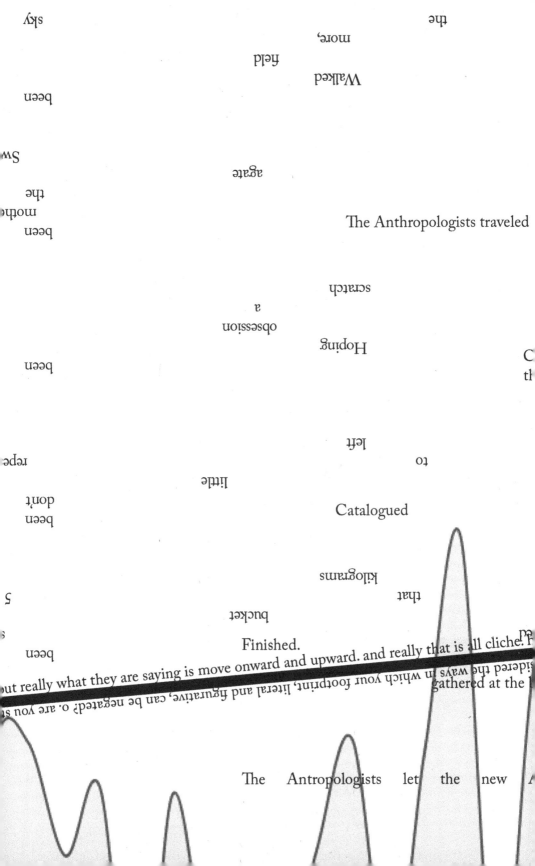

sky

the

more,

field

Walked

been

Sw

agate

the

moth

been

The Anthropologists traveled

scratch

a

obsession

Hoping

been

C

th

left

to

repe

little

don't

been

Catalogued

kilograms

that

bucket

5

been

Finished.

but really what they are saying is move onward and upward. and really that is all cliche. I

sidered the ways in which your footprint, literal and figurative, can be negated? o. are you s

gathered at the

The   Antropologists   let   the   new

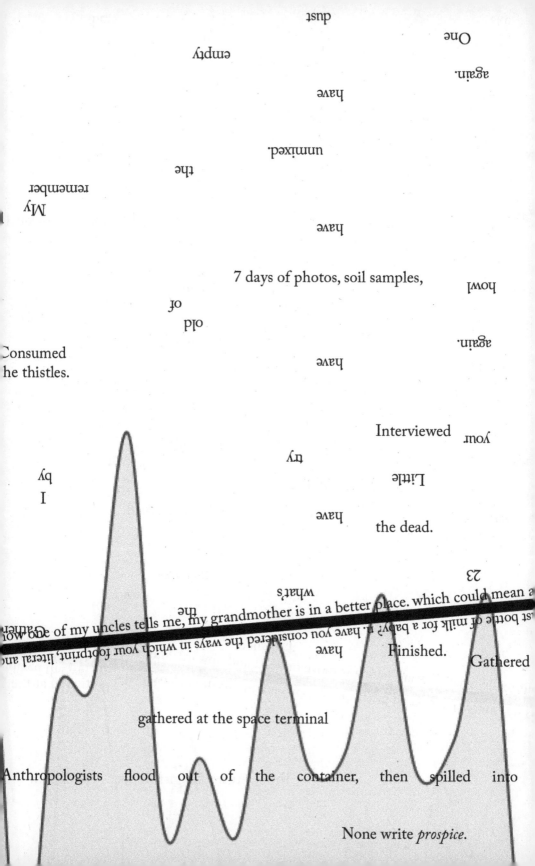

dust

One

empty

again.

have

unmixed.

the

My remember

have

7 days of photos, soil samples,

howl

of
old

Consumed
he thistles.

have

again.

Interviewed   your

try

Little

by
I

have

the dead.

23

what's

One of my uncles tells me, my grandmother is in a better place. which could mean a
the
st bottle of milk for a baby? n. have you considered the ways in which your footprint, literal and
low one of my uncles tells me, the
ue literal footprint,   Gradmother

have   Finished.   Gathered

gathered at the space terminal

Anthropologists   flood   out   of   the   container,   then   spilled   into

None write *prospice*.

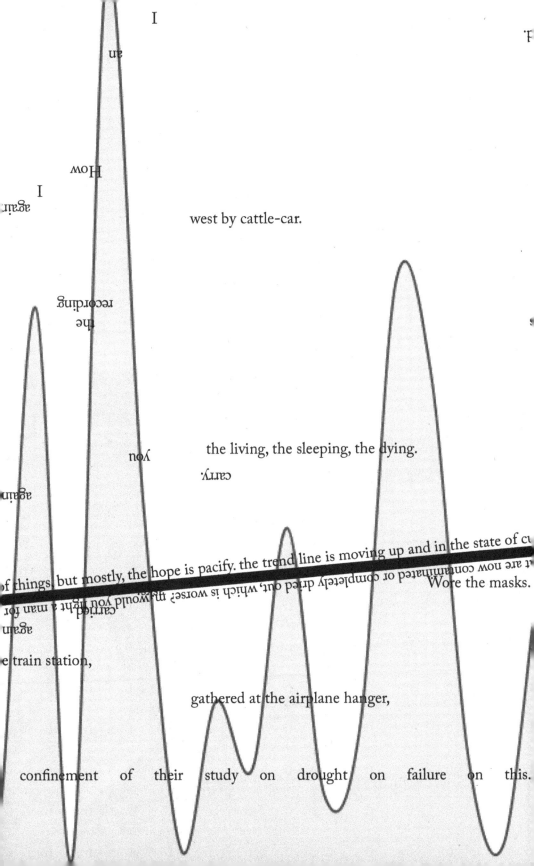

I

F.

an

How

I

again

west by cattle-car.

recording
the

you

the living, the sleeping, the dying.

carry.

again

of things but mostly, the hope is pacify. the trend line is moving up and in the state of cu
t are now contaminated or completely dried out, which is worse? m would you fight a man for
carried you would fi
Wore the masks.

again

e train station,

gathered at the airplane hanger,

confinement   of   their   study   on   drought   on   failure   on   this.

oiceinternal

file://
marigold-
factory.png/
eachdoor-
blownopen-
>>>nside_the_1s_and_0s_convert///
toexposethe->an_ocular_recollection.exe//
othercolor

>>>>>>>>>apply_the_self_as_x.exe/
click_thru_and_enter_portal.exe///

file://
png/wake-
worksleep-
routine.

sleepwake-
wakework-
worksleep-
sleepwake-
wakesleep-
workstep-
wakesleep
>>download_landscape_//

HTTP 404 - File not found

run_familiarity_sequence.exe////

file://here.
png/as-
tainedcarpe-
torcoffeecu-
poranalumi-
numsutured-
wound

file://vari
ation.png/
undefinedre-
fractionsof-
light

I
agate of
skyward.
lands.

I
remain
boots. and
agate I

grit
feld
replaces
agate
I

why
saying,
I
agate
I

answer.
would
man
and
agate
I

current economies it combusts actuarialists to see these peaks are now off the page at pr

eep adaptation to climate change, i might not be rhetorical, so which watershed would

"Inasmuch as I am in the land, it is appropriate that I should affirm myself in the spirit of the land. I shall celebrate my life in the world, and the world in my life. In the natural order man invests himself in the landscape and at the same time incorporates the landscape into his own most fundamental experience. This trust is sacred."

— N. Scott Momaday

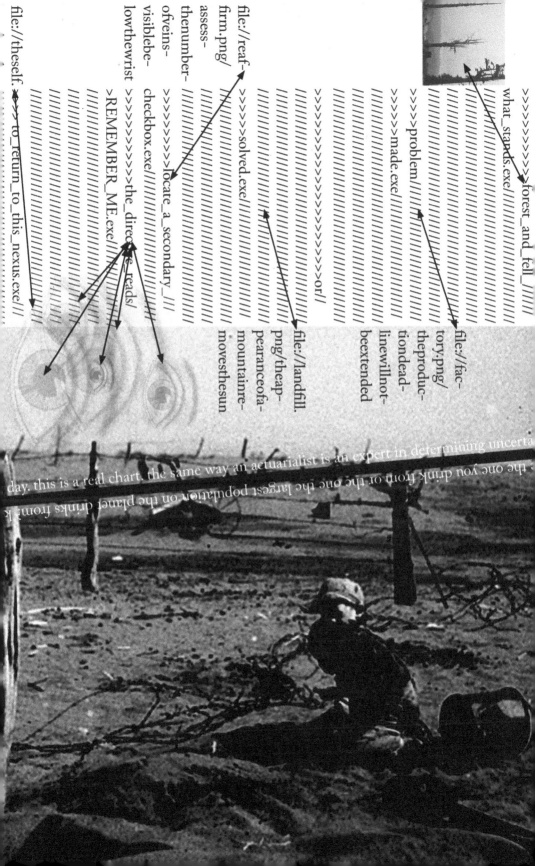

file://theself.>>>to_return_to_this_nexus.exe//

file://reaf-firm.png/

assess-thenumber-ofveins-visiblebe-lowthewrist

>>>>>>checkbox.exe//

>REMEMBER_ME.exe//

>>>>>>>>>>the_directive_reads/

>>>>>>>>locate_a_secondary_//

file://solved.exe////

file://landfill.png/theap-pearanceofa-mountainre-movesthesun

>>>>>>>>>>>>>>>>or/

>>>>>>>>>>problem////made.exe////

>>>>>problem/theproduc-tiondead-linewillnot-beextended

file://fac-tory.png/

what_stands.exe//>>>>>>>>>>forest_and_fell_//

day. this is a real chart. the same way an actuarialist is an expert in determining uncerta

the one you drink from or the one the largest population on the planet drinks from? k

file://wan-
ingcrescent.
png/how-
roundthe-
shadow

file://swal-
low.png/
whatgoe-
sawayarrive-
selsewhere

>>>>>>>>>>>>>>the_curvature_of_//

>>>>>down_the_storm_drain.exe////

>>>>>pour_motor_oil_down////

>chrome_the_dual_exhaust/

>>>>>exhaust_idle_the_truck_all_///
afternoon.exe///////////////////

>>>>>assemble_the_garbage_///
into_a_pile///////////////

>>>pile_and_set_peak_on_fire.exe//

>>>>>>>>>>>>take_the_blade_to_a_forest/
>>>>>>>>>>>>forest_and_fell /////

file://pla-
neofemi-
nence.png/
awaitin-
gandnever-
arriving

file://yawn.
png/dar-
ingthe-
sunlight
tore-
main

file://anew-
mountain.
png/growin-
guntilthesun
muzzles

unconraminated? }. if you could cleanse and deconraminate one watershed, would it be
tainty and risk. and in the state of current economies, reward. the actuarialist studies the

until upright

provides the Ma

Speak to the spine, the l
Speak bone. Spe
Bone.

Offspring
learn – lean.

forward...
affirm_I'M_NOT_A_ROBOT.exe//////
>>>>>>>>via_checkbox.exe////////

file://af-
firmation.
png/con-
vinceyour-
selfatsunris-
esunsetre-
peat
>>>>>>but_I_find_myself///////////
>>>>>>>>>>distracted_///
>>>>>>>that_is_an_incomplete///

file://con-
firmation.
png/
tongues.
png/silen-
ceinthe-
blogosphere

file://
tongues.
png/silen-
ceinthe-
blogosphere
>this_is_the_gap_in_the_
conversation_model.exe//////

file://
image.png/
>the_circular_arrows_//////////
never_touch.exe//

file://stock-
image.png/

file://confir-
mation.png
>>REDUCE_REUSE_
RECYCLE_///LOGO.exe///////
meanit

by_the_symbol////////////////

Science

expectancy of both the financial and the living things leaning upon the about life expect
aptation - how will you tell the tangible goodbye? i, have you considered the taste of w

Orang}   Chimpanzee}   Gorilla}

Chimpanzee}
Man}Gibbon}
Gibbon}
Orang}

apply plow.   ~~Indigenous~~
               ~~Grass~~
               ~~Topsoil~~
               ~~Roots~~
               New here.

he femur. Speak to the spine, the hip, the femur. Speak to the spine, the hip, the fem
one. Speak bone. Speak bone. Speak bone. Speak bone. Speak bone. Speak bone. Spe

Bone.   Bone.   Bone.   Bone.

     And   lean.

          Call this:
          development.   Call this:
                                  advancement.

107

(A storm births an egg vacuums open a thirsting.)   And here, we c

dr fndr

th frtnt chld ws tld cnsm fstr

s th frtnt cnsmd fstr

cnsmd t dbl spd ll th dt nd nfrmtn

ws fld

mgn fld

wth ll th drght nd blzng

lk t ll tht mpty

tll m

nt f th lngth f th rd bt hw frgt w fst hrzn hw rmmbr w

fst

rspctflly

x

...ancy we are really saying that people are looking at how long we will live and how muc...

...hen was the last moment that something was pulled from your hands? h. in the deep ac...

has traced:

Gorilla}<

Man}

Man Gibbon}<   Orang}<   Chimpanzee}<   Gorilla}<

and acreage

...ur. Speak to the spine, the hip, the femur. Speak to the spine, the hip, the femur.
...ak bone. Speak bone. Speak bone. Speak bone. Speak bone. Speak bone. Speak bone.

Bone.   Bone.   Bone.   Bone.

Further. Further.

Call this: progress.

all this destiny.

"There is no problem from CO$_2$. The world has lots and lots of problems, but increasing CO$_2$ is not one of the problems."

-William Happer, formerly U.S. Nat'l Security Council director on emerging technologies

ing we will do while alive and if so, what does a future life look like with a trend line th[

[va]lue? what do you value? f. what can you relinquish? have you tested your grip strength?

Man}

i am talking loud again, as i sigh and cuss at an entire bag of fast food garbage being thrown out a car window as the we both loop onto the highway. it explodes on the road and i see the contents bloomspew. there was ice in the cup and it gleams with the headlights of traffic behind me. i am mad at the self - saying this ice is beauty. i am mad at the driver and see they have a blue lives matter sticker in their window. i speed up to see and pass them. before i honk i realize it is my neighbor. an old white man who married a young mexican woman. he speaks no spanish. while doing yardwork he blares conservative talkradio conspiracy theorists on a handheld am radio. we are both on our way home. the same neighbor who, during halloween, gave out pre-packed candy bags that contained several whole candy bars and a message from a nearby church that read: are you ready for the end times?

eak bone.

"[T]his humpback was found near the mouth of the Amazon River, some 4,000 miles from its expected feeding grounds, a baffling discovery that has stumped the scientists who found it."

-Feb. 25, 2019 NYT article regarding a humpback beached in Brazil, 50 feet from water

in the anthropocene:

adjective::different
noun::static

at continues ascension? a futurism of expansion finds a cliff and recedes, unlike the rive

nd of the chimes? d. will you be able to write in the shape of those chimes? e. what is v

v is t? c. what is the shape of those chimes? d.

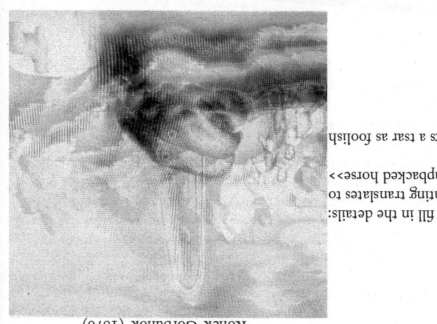

"Konek-Gorbunok" (1870)

fill in the details:
eeing this painting translates to
<<little humpbacked horse>>

which depicts a tsar as foolish

no one attempts to explain the existence

        of monster
        of ghost
        of villain

noun::human

...es, and oceans. a futurism of invention, not of brilliance, but from the necessity of survi...

...d remember you will .c etirw dna niaga erutplucs eciov eht ot netsil uoy lliw .b ?secihpy

exert ache to swim upearth to father's hill humpback
return to watchwitness humpback
return to airspew humpback
return to gritted teeth humpback
return to the eye humpback
less so polar bear

see whale   not knowing this as poem by yershov

Poll Question:
Should I be more or less angry, if my neighbor had thrown a bag of
trash into my own backyard instead of on the highway on-ramp?

☐ More angry - 50%

☐ Less angry, you can clean it up - 3%

☐ Confront him, what else does he do when no one is watching - 47%

☐ None of the above, it is all backyard - 0%

survival. someone will say survival is the necessity of invention.

a. will you listen to bit.ly/VoiceSculptureANeoapocalypt

but i accept the omission of man

An old man chooses to print the internet un-alt'r-ed for a photo album he will raise upon his alt'r.

The living fail to recognize the concept of infinite, and soon there are no canopies for a rain forest alt'r.

Progeny of progeny of progeny wither watching the patience of a print queue to assemblage alt'r.

In the ancient, anthropologists learn, a single fence post for a diocese of desert is the only place for others to alt'r.

At a yard sale, a man buys an incomplete photo album, fills pages with "Self-Portrait, in Drought", makes himself alt'r.

Near Wetumka, OK, another man proclaims the Dust Bowl is a novena to recite into the tendons of the alt'r.

In thirst, the first thing that vacates the body, is voice, and how do I dismantle when all that remains is alt'r?

112

brd

stdnt sks

    hw s th flyng thng splld?

tchr sys

    ll th sft lttrs hv blwn ff
    spll brd

                  lk   brd

tchr tlls stry

    frst mnfst dstny
    th bffl wr hntd nd skltns stckd
    th ntv ppl wr pshd n slghtrd

    tk wht th y cn s

    thn crps plntd nd plntd nd plntd nd plntd
    thn dry nd ht nd dry nd cld nd dry nd ht
    thn rbbts nd rbbts nd rbbts
    thn mn clbbd ll th rbbts
    pld nd lghd
    vrythng brnd
    ll th ppl thrstd nd th lnd crckd
    brd jst lft bfr snrs nd snst
    brd dsspprd
    thn nsts mpty

stdnt sks

    wht hppnd t brd?

tchr sys

    brd sys n brnchs t prch nd crps cllps
    nd hrvsts nd n wrms s hngry

    brd sys spk sky   spk   drk spk

ll thngs trnd psdwn
stdnt sks

                                                thn blw
                                                wy

nd trnds nd hrrcns nd wrs nd dss
nd nthng lvng

stdnt sks
        dd brd knw?

tchr nswrs
        brd knw   trd t spk
                        thrt splt

        brd ndd wtr

stdnt sys
        whts wtr?

stll lf

th cns r fll f snkn thngs:
        xtnct nml skltns
        hmn crcsss: grwn n chld
        cffns tht wr hss
        brbd wr fr nvr blt wlls

nc   whl wnt t th cn nd dv nt th dpst prts fnd thr
             fthr nd mthr bt bns dsntgrt

mgn   whl bllnnng thr ncstrs

nw   whl ws dvsttd   t tk n th lv nd crd

whl   crd fr twnty svn mnths nd th slnty f th cn grw
             nd slt hrdns r drs t snd

lstn   tht cn ws thrsty
             gspng gspng ntl sld nd slnt

whl   nw wlks n wht ws n cn
             lss mrcls
             mr stll drsl pryr

dr fndr – th frtnt chld prvrb

dr fndr

n th pst

th frtnt chld

        nvr hrd
        hst mks wst

hw fst w frgt th rt f cclrtn

s fst   w kpt mvng mvng mvng   n spc t brth ntl w bncd ff
                chthr ntl w cld n lngr mv frly
                ntl sky trns nt skybl

                fndr
                r y nw th frtnt chld
        f s   pry gd strks y dwn
                smk brl nd shllw grv

                                s fst y hrdly brth
                                s fst y hrdly brth
                                s fst y hrdly brth
                                s fst y hrdly brth
                                s fst y hrdly brth
                                s fst y hrdly brth
                                s fst y hrdly brth
                      hw fst w mk nly t dsppr

sncrly
x

dr fndr – th frtnt chld nd whl

dr fndr,

r y wll?

f y r rdng ths r w stll brthng xygn r thr?

wht d y mk f r rndrng?

pls frgv m skng s mny qstns   ll stp

pls jst trst ths nfrmtn   th frtnt chld ds nt wlk nt th whl blly
                                           nd srvvs n fsh nd bl
                                           n n wlks nt th whl blly nd srvvs
        tng th fsh   drnkng th bld   tstng
        th lvng   n lvng
                             wll mt   rfrncs
                                                       th bbl
                                                       th bbls
                                                       r nw bhnd glss
n lss stdd

        dr fndr   ths s nt bt rlgn
                                   nsmch s t s bt th rcrd
                                   f mmry   nd wh wlks nt th blly

    thnkng thy wll wlk bck nt dylght

    dr fndr
    whtvr rmns frm th grwth
    r nt th vcs n yr hd bt skn
    f wht pls nd pls ntl nthng

    dr fndr
    hw snst prvds hp bt nvr rspt

    fndr
    hw wtnss n th drk rmmbrs th shp f llmntn

                                                       x

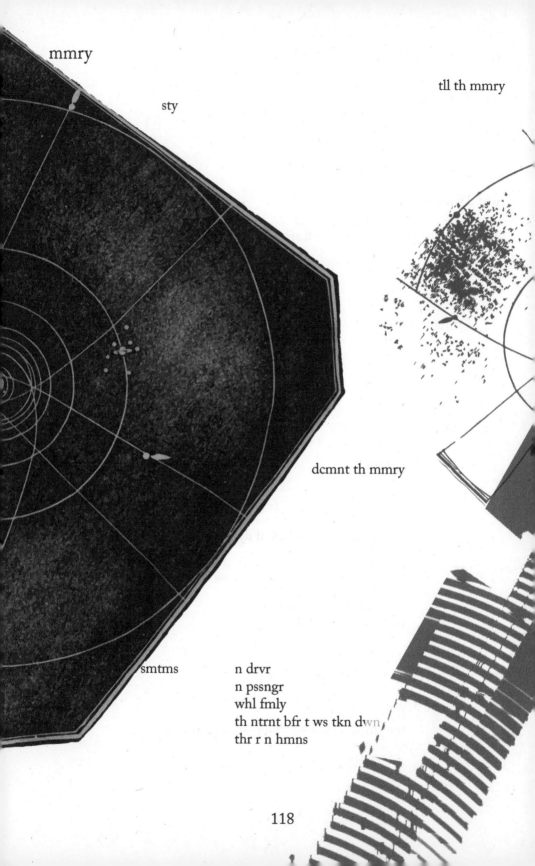

mmry

sty

tll th mmry

dcmnt th mmry

smtms

n drvr
n pssngr
whl fmly
th ntrnt bfr t ws tkn dwn
thr r n hmns

drvng gsln
vhcl th drvr wtnsss
hrs s n fld
f drt t ds nt gllp
bt s stll th hd s tght
gnst th rbs nd th drvr cnts
ch 1 t 11 bfr pssng th drvr sks
th pssngr dd y s th frl
hrs hw th bns lkd brttl
nd wtng t snp th pssngr crs
t th mgn nd t stys wth thm
lkng t th strt snppd fmr
n Pgss nt th drk f frst
flln lg hrss tslf drng th strms
ths hvs lsswght dsppr
n th prtclt th fld s mpty

dcmn t
dcmn t
dcmnt
dc mn
dcmn t

lwys crtr tchng mmry n whtvr prsnt
n hw t cntn wht ws nc lvng nd s nw nt nw
hw t stry th tmrrw n th ystrdy?

wtr

th   bgnnng   ws   wtr.   wtr

flld   th   cns   nd   gthrd

n   th   clds.   thr   ws   rn

fr   crps   nd   thrst.

th   flds   rvrd   nd   gt   hghr

tl   th   chldrn   cldnt   swm

tl   th   hrs   nd   chckn   swllwd

th   wtr.   hw   rth   cnsms

vrythng.   hw   rth   brns

bck.   thr   s   nthng.   whl

bchs   tslf.   bchs   tslf.   bchs

tslf   tll   th   ppl   t   stp.   ppl

dnt   stp.   thy   mk   wrs.

ys   thr   s   wtr.   nd   nn   cn   swm.

whl

th stry dsnt bgn
w   n th bgnnng   th stry nvr bgns
                                          whls nvr rd bbls

nw hstrns wll lctr   n th shttrd schls ths s wht hppns
                        t th gdlss

            bt ll th clssrms   r clsd

                                                    chld
                                                              dr
                                                    chld
                                              yr   frtnt
                                              yr   whl
              nd wlkng wy

nt   frst   nd brth wht y wsh   tdy   cll yr fmly nm
                        sk sky
                  t bl vn fr mnt

chld
                                                              dr
                                                    chld
                                              yr   frtnt
                                              yr   whl

                        nd hm s hr nt thr   hr
              sng

              sng

        t slp

cnt th ncstrs

                              wh
                              ddnt wtnss th lvng fl

slt wndw

Dr fndr

Th thrshlds r sld
N th lng slp f nvr wkng knw
tht slt wndws xst
D nt clmb n   nstd tng th slt glss
Dhydrtn brngs th vsn

Bynd th wndw
Pn f ll rds tht hv frkd
Trn snk tng hssng snlght
Prss t t yr mth
tst th knwng f gnshng tdl wvs

V
/\

////ftr th trs////th lvng strtd cllng chnlnk fnc psts tr////////////////
//thr wr mny///
////////ntl chnlnk fnc psts trnd cmmdty/////////////////////////////
//lstn/////////////////
///
/////////////////////////////////t s nt mttr f rvng//////////////////////

/////////////y sk wht s rvg//
/thr s n nswr///
///th slf s lrnng/////////////
///
/////////////th scrp f shdw////////////////////////////////~~////////////////
///wtht shd//////////

//////////ftr lrnng wlll b mbddd n th dtbdy crps/////////////////////
/////////////////////////th crps plntd/////////////////////////////////
//////whn th dst b///
/////////////////////////////th bns////////////////////////////////

/////////////////////////n th ftr////////////////////ths s lllby////////////

/////////twnklng str/////////////crdls fr//////////////////////////////
//hw//////////////////lght////////
////////////scrms/////////////////////////wntng clm///////////////////

/
\

Communique 1.3.0.b - The Ancestral Progeny of Megaptera Novaeangliae

{held you i once}

{beached}

{sciencecoronerincision pressed index|middle|ring wound & sob}

{spinal exposure
column}

{say scientists disoriented mammalian blunt force wreckage}

{say internets lesssight tree}

{once held i you}

{waves i watched wish you home wish you home wish you home}

{lessrelent more nessrestfull}

{tell now}

{>|</>|</>|</>|</>|<}

{lied man a once}

{lessrelent more nessrestfull}

{bucketboiled himself}

{all bucketboiled all}

{called ok all}

{all gone}

{lessrelent more nessrestfull}

{all you}

{this be home}

{stop}

{lessrelent more nessrestfull}

{be this home}

{stop}

{lessrelent more no wardhome}

{this}

{you held once i}

{begin}

{you all}

{this}

{wardsky landhome nessrestfull}

Notes

"Cada día más cerca del fin del Mundo": The illustration utilized is a digitized and destroyed photograph of a logging machine.

"Examination of Ruin": The photographs sourced in the poem were discovered in a tool box at a thrift store in Fresno, CA, and bundled together with a piece of string.

"U.S. Weather Bureau Report Monthly Report, February 1935": The redactions and found texts are related to the United States Weather Bureau's report. Portions of which can be accessed at https://ia800309.us.archive.org/1/items/yoa1935/yoa1935.pdf.

"It was conditions of this sort which forced many farmers to abandon the area, Spring '35, New Mexico": Is a title from a Dorothea Lange photograph. The image can be accessed at https://lccn.loc.gov/2017759935.

"The Basilica of Dust": The photograph was taken by Dorothea Lange and titled "A corral practically buried by drifted dust. Mills, New Mexico. Therefore, the fertile top soil of a grazing area cannot be utilized." The photograph was accessed via the Library of Congress's archive. The image is in the public. The image can be accessed at https://lccn.loc.gov/2017759937.

"Solitude; Or, Along a California highway, A Dust Bowl Refugee": The photograph was taken by Dorothea Lange and titled "Along a California highway, a dust bowl refugee bound for Oregon." The photograph was accessed via the Library of Congress's archive. The image is in the public domain. The image can be accessed at https://lccn.loc.gov/2017769814.

"This land is your land, Holtville, California": The photograph was taken by Dorothea Lange and titled "Refugee families encamped near Holtville, California." The photograph was accessed via the Library of Congress's archive. The image is in the public domain. The image can be accessed at https://lccn.loc.gov/2017769770. Additionally, the opening portion in italics is in reference to Woody Guthrie's song, "This Land Is Your Land".

"A Dust Bowl Field Recording, Arvin, CA, 1940": The poem is in conversation of the oral histories of the Dust Bowl. The audio recording can be accessed at https://www.loc.gov/item/toddbib000002.

"Nothing but a Margin, But a Yield": The photograph, which I edited by breaking it into small circles via graphic design software, is from the George E. Marsh album and titled "Dust Storm Texas 1935." The photograph was accessed via Wikipedia Commons. It is in the public domain with no known copyright restriction because it contains materials that originally came from the U.S. National Oceanic and Atmospheric Administration. Additionally, all lines that are on arcs are epigraphs from Woody Guthrie's album "Dust Bowl Ballads," songs Guthrie wrote after visiting the areas impacted by the Dust Bowl. Specifically, referenced are "The Great Dust Storm (Dust Storm Disaster)," "I Ain't Got No Home in This World Anymore," "Dust Can't Kill Me," "Dust Pneumonia Blues," "Do Re Mi," and "Dusty Old Dust." Lastly, portions of the United Nations' Intergovernmental Panel on Climate Change special report titled "Global Warming of 1.5 ºC" are referenced in the poem. The report can be accessed at https://www.ipcc.ch/sr15/.

"Everywhere I Sleep, I see Dust Bowl 1.0": The photograph was taken by Dorothea Lange and titled "Oklahoma mother of five children, now picking cotton in California, near Fresno." The photograph was accessed via the Library of Congress's archive. The image is in the public domain. The image can be accessed at https://lccn.loc.gov/2017763199. The cascading effect in the photo was augmented via a graphic design program by the author.

"Everywhere I Sleep, I see Dust Bowl 2.0": The photograph was taken by Dorothea Lange and is titled "Between Tulare and Fresno on U.S. 99. Highway gas tanks and signboard approaching town." The photograph was accessed via the Library of Congress's archive. The image is in the public. The image can be accessed at https://lccn.loc.gov/2017771971.

"Everywhere I Sleep, I see Dust Bowl 3.0": The poem is in conversation with a stereograph taken by John P. Soule and is titled "Big tree, felled in Frezno [sic] Grove, (78 ft. circum.) Frezno [sic] Co." The stereograph was accessed via the New York Public Library's Digital Collection. To access the stereograph visit - https://digitalcollections.nypl.org/items/510d47e2-5902-a3d9-e040-e00a18064a99.

"Everywhere I Sleep, I see Dust Bowl 4.0": The poem references a Library of Congress archival interview of Dust Bowl Refugee Charlie Spurlock in Arvin, CA on July 28, 1940. The interview, in its entirety, can be accessed at https://www.loc.gov/item/toddbib000003/.

"Everywhere I Sleep, I see Dust Bowl 5.0": The photograph was taken by Dorothea Lange and is titled "Migrants' tents are a common sight along the right of way of the Southern Pacific. Near Fresno, California" The photograph was accessed via the Library of Congress's archive. The image is in the public. The image can be accessed at https://lccn.loc.gov/2017771611.

"Everywhere I Sleep, I see Dust Bowl 6.0": The photograph was taken by Dorothea Lange and is titled "Highway City, California, near Fresno. See general caption. Family from Oklahoma; have been in California for six years, have been migratory workers now on Works Progress Administration from which they may be cut off at the opening of the 1939 harvest." The photograph was accessed via the Library of Congress's archive. The image is in the public. The image can be accessed at https://lccn.loc.gov/2017771948. The image utilizes both the back of the photograph, as well as a portion of a fence in the photograph, and was augmented via a graphic design program by the author.

"Everywhere I Sleep, I see Dust Bowl 7.0": The photograph was taken by Dorothea Lange and is titled "Between Tulare and Fresno on U.S. 99. See general caption. Family inspect a house trailer with idea of purchase." The photograph was accessed via the Library of Congress's archive. The image is in the public domain and can be accessed at https://lccn.loc.gov/2017771983. The cascading effect in the photo was augmented via a graphic design program by the author.

"Everywhere I Sleep, I see Dust Bowl 8.0": The photograph was taken by Dorothea Lange and is titled "Irrigation pump on edge of field. Electric power typical of San Joaquin Valley farming. California." The photograph was accessed via the Library of Congress's archive. The image is in the public domain. The image can be accessed at https://lccn.loc.gov/2017770867.

"Everywhere I Sleep, I see Dust Bowl 9.0": The photograph was taken by Dorothea Lange and titled "On the plains west of Fresno, California. Family of seven from Oregon dairy ranch which they lost. 'We tried to get too big, I guess. Milk cans are all that's left of the dairy. Now pick bolls to make fifty cents to one dollar a day.'" The photograph was accessed via the Library of Congress's archive. The image is in the public domain. The image can be accessed at https://lccn.loc.gov/2017771257.

"Everywhere I Sleep, I see Dust Bowl 10.0": The photograph was taken by Dorothea Lange and is titled "Car trouble on west side of Highway No. 33 in San Joaquin Valley. Formerly a California cowhand and roving laborer. Now with his wife, he follows the fruit. 'My uncle homesteaded here sixty years ago. I'm lower on money than at any time.'" The photograph was accessed via the Library of Congress's archive. The image is in the public domain. The image can be accessed at https://lccn.loc.gov/2017770686.

"Everywhere I Sleep, I see Dust Bowl 11.0": The photograph was taken by Dorothea Lange and is titled "Fresno. On U.S. 99. Storefront of San Joaquin Valley town. California." The photograph was accessed via the Library of Congress's archive. The image is in the public domain. The image can be accessed at https://lccn.loc.gov/2017772005. The effects on the photo were augmented via a graphic design program by the author.

"Everywhere I Sleep, I see Dust Bowl 12.0": The photograph was taken by Dorothea Lange and titled "U.S. 99 on ridge over Tehachapi Mountains. Heavy truck route between Los Angeles and San Joaquin Valley over which migrants travel back and forth. California." The photograph was accessed via the Library of Congress's archive. The image is in the public domain. The image can be accessed at https://lccn.loc.gov/2017771926. The effects on the photo were augmented via a graphic design program by the author.

"Everywhere I Sleep, I see Dust Bowl 13.0": The postcard was issued by the Detroit Publishing Company. The title of the postcard is "Oil Wells, Fresno, Calif." The photograph was accessed via the New York Public Library's Digital Collection. It is in the public domain with no known copyright restriction. To access the postcard that is referenced, visit - https://digitalcollections.nypl.org/items/510d47d9-a520-a3d9-e040-e00a18064a99.

"Everywhere I Sleep, I see Dust Bowl 14.0": The poem is in conversation with the stereograph produced by Underwood and Underwood and is titled "Ending a life of centuries, a giant tree falling, logging among the big trees, Converse Basin, California." The photograph was accessed via the New York Public Library's Digital Collection. To access the stereograph visit - https://digitalcollections.nypl.org/items/510d47e2-5924-a3d9-e040-e00a18064a99#/?uuid=510d47e2-5924-a3d9-e040-e00a18064a99.

"Everywhere I Sleep, I see Dust Bowl 15.0": The photograph was taken by Dorothea Lange and is titled "Employment signs in Spanish and English. These ranches (1938) increasingly use Negro pickers. Near Fresno, California." The photograph was accessed via the Library of Congress's archive. The image is in the public domain. The image can be accessed at https://lccn.loc.gov/2017760263. The effects on the photo were augmented via a graphic design program by the author for each depiction.

"Analog Jaguar Digitization Forest Canopy": were sourced from a series of photographs by Eadweard Muybridge titled "Jaguar walking then turning around" first published in 1887 at Philadelphia (Animal Locomotion). It is in the public domain with no known copyright restrictions.

"Elements of a Dust Bowl Field Recording": The poem was inspired by an archival recording from the Library of Congress interview of Dust Bowl Refugee Charlie Spurlock in Arvin, CA on July 28, 1940. The interview, in its entirety, can be accessed at https://www.loc.gov/item/toddbib000003/.

"In a Season": This poem is inspired by Audre Lorde.

"In Watching Tiny Tim's "The Ice Caps are Melting" (1968) I Understand": The poem is inspired by a Tiny Tim performance, which can be viewed on YouTube at https://www.youtube.com/watch?v=uAZgTKsdJsc.

"Megadrought, DustLore1.5°c": Portions of the United Nations' Intergovernmental Panel on Climate Change special report titled "Global Warming of 1.5 °C" are referenced in the poem. The report can be accessed at https://www.ipcc.ch/sr15/.

"A Neoapocalyptices": The large central photograph was taken by Arthur Rothstein in April 1936. The title of the photograph is "Dust bowl farmer raising fence to keep it from being buried under drifting sand. Cimarron County, Oklahoma." The photograph was accessed via the Library of Congress. It is in the public domain with no known copyright restriction. The image can be accessed at https://lccn.loc.gov/2017760334/. The photograph, "Dust storm. It was conditions of this sort which forced many farmers to abandon the area. Spring 1935. New Mexico" was taken by Dorothea Lange. The photograph was accessed via the New York Public Library's Public Domain Archive. It is in the public domain with no known copyright restriction. The photograph can be accessed at https://digitalcollections. nypl.org/items/dab42b70-73ef-0136-3655-1df4c6917cc4. The illustration titled "Konek Gorbunok" is by an unknown author. This work is in the public domain in its country of origin and other countries and areas where the copyright term is the author's life plus 100 years or fewer. This file has been identified as being free of known restrictions under copyright law, including all related and neighboring rights. The image can be accessed from Wikipedia Commons at https://commons.wikimedia.org/wiki/File:Konek_ Gorbunok_1870.jpg. Lastly, the poem along the trendline features a reference to a voice sculpture, the voice sculpture is portions of Jem Bendell's study on the climate collapse/catastrophe "Deep Adaptation," sourced from Bendell's own reading at https://soundcloud.com/user-56712817/deep-adaptation (the report can also be accessed at http://www.lifeworth.com/deepadaptation.

pdf), as well as my own recording of a Spring 2019 storm in my backyard. The voice sculpture can be accessed at http://anthonycody.com/wp-content/uploads/2020/02/DeepAdaptation.mp3.

"Mmry": The illustration is titled "Edward Wallace; or, the little astronomer" and the author is unknown. The image's style was augmented by the author via graphic design software. To access the illustration visit - https://digitalcollections.lib.washington.edu/digital/collection/childrens/id/904. It is in the public domain with no known copyright restriction. The effects on the image were augmented via a graphic design program by the author.

"Wtr": The illustration is by William Daniell and titled "Whale." The image's style was augmented by the author via graphic design software. The image was accessed via the New York Public Library's Digital Collection. It is in the public domain with no known copyright restriction. To access the illustration visit - https://digitalcollections.nypl.org/items/510d47d9-52ad-a3d9-e040-e00a18064a99.

Extending the Poem

The QR Codes and sound file referenced in "Nothing but a Margin, but a Yield" and "a Neoapocalyptices" can be found on Omnidawn's website, as of April 2023, at https://www.omnidawn.com/extending-the-poem-from-the-rendering/ and http://anthonycody.com/TheRendering.

Acknowledgements

Deep admiration, love, and respect to: The Yokuts, Mono, Washoe, Peoria, Potawatomi, and Miami peoples, on whose occupied territory I have lived, been nourished by in the making of this collection.

~

My appreciation to the editors and curators of the following publications in which earlier versions of these poems first appeared:

Poetry: "Cada día más cerca del fin del Mundo"

Magma Poetry (UK): "Analog Jaguar Digitization Forest Canopy"

The Colorado Review: "wtr" and "Elegy with Barbed Wire Swaddling a Fortunate Child, as Barded Triptych Assemblage"

The Academy of American Poets, Poem-a-Day Series: "brd" and "'Stop, go put your shoes back on. They'll know we Okies,' a Lost Image Reclamation."

FresnoWriters.Com: Portions of "Everywhere I sleep, I see Dust Bowl"

Anomaly: "DustLore35"

ctrl+v journal: "This land is your land, Holtville, California"

Elderly Mag: "A Dust Bowl Field Recording, Arvin, CA, 1940," "Communique 1.3.0.b - The Ancestral Progeny of Megaptera Novaeangliae," "Everywhere I sleep, I see Dust Bowl, 13.0," "In watching Tiny Tim's 'The Ice Caps Are Melting' (1968) I understand," and "mmry"

SOMArts: "a Neoapocalyptices" and "Nothing but a Margin, but a Yield" were originally staged and exhibited in the Ramp Gallery in San Franciscso, CA, Spring 2022 at SOMArts.

~

This collection would not be possible without the care and consideration of my time in the spaces and people within those spaces that have sustained me: Laureate Lab Visual Words Studio, CantoMundo, Community of Writers, Hmong American Writers' Circle, Randolph College, El Taller Latino Americano, Fresno State, and Fresno.

The majority of this collection was written prior to the pandemic, yet my friendships (old and new) have nourished me in ways that continue to help me meet the page, revise the work, and move through the world both gently and viciously. My deepest appreciation to Juan Felipe Herrera, Carmen Giménez, Farid Matuk, Douglas Kearney, Keith S. Wilson, J.J. Hernandez, Mariah Bosch, Javier Lopez, Chevas Clements, Paul Sanchez, Rebeca Flores, Andre Yang, Hermelinda Hernandez Monjaras, Soul Vang, Burlee Vang, Pos L. Moua (QEPD), Ángel García, Rigoberto González, Eduardo C. Corral, Russell Morse, Josue Rojas, Bernardo Palombo, giovanni singleton, Suzi F. Garcia, Sarah Gzemski, Diana Arterian, Roberto Tejada, Joshua Escobar, Vanessa A. Villarreal, Jasminne Mendez, Mei-mei Berssenbrugge, Sara Borjas, Joseph Rios, David Campos, Steven Sanchez, Juan Luis Guzman, Khaty Xiong, Diana Khoi Nguyen, Josiah Luis Alderete, Marcelo Hernandez Castillo, Javier Zamora, George Abraham, Ángel Dominguez, Sheila Maldonado, Raquel Salas Rivera, Lupe Mendez, Francisco Aragón, David Tomas Martinez, Manuel Paul Lopez, Ruben Quesada, Roda Avelar, Brynn Saito, Connie Hales, and countless others for their presence on the path.

Much love to Susan Briante, Daniel Borzutzky, and Douglas Kearney for diving into the collection and gifting the work with their deep seeing.

My unending admiration to the team at Omnidawn – Rusty, Ken (QEPD), Rob, Laura, and the omniverse of authors; thinking and working alongside each of you is a mobius strip of joy.

To Delorse, Isabel, Walter, and Antonio (my late-grandparents), and my parents, Mary and Douglas, you have taught me the grind, laid the foundations, resisted the narrative, and I know we must keep dreaming and scheming for ourselves.

To Mai Der Vang, my dearest love, to meet the sunrise together, journey toward each full moon, and re-imagine the possibilities of the epic poem that is our life is a perpetual gift.

This book is dedicated to my nieces and nephews: Leilani, Landon, Carter, Ryan, Matthew, Gwen, Dara, Charlotte, Wesley, Vincent, Madison, Sophie, and those still to come, I know a better way is possible because I have seen it and it is you.

Author bio:

Anthony Cody is the author of *Borderland Apocrypha* (Omnidawn, 2020), winner of the 2018 Omnidawn Open Book Prize, selected by the poet Mei-mei Berssenbrugge. His debut collection has been honored as a 2022 Whiting Award winner, a 2021 American Book Award winner, a 2020 Southwest Book Award winner, a 2020 *Poets & Writers* debut poet, as well as a finalist for the National Book Award, a PEN America / Jean Stein Award, a L.A. Times Book Award, a California Book Award, and longlisted for a Believer Magazine Editor's award. He is a CantoMundo fellow from Fresno, California with lineage in the Bracero Program and the Dust Bowl.

His poems have appeared in The Academy of American Poets: *Poem-A-Day Series*, *Poetry*, *Gulf Coast*, *Ninth Letter*, *Prairie Schooner*, *The Colorado Review*, UK's *Magma Poetry* (UK), *TriQuarterly*, *ctrl+v journal*, among others. Anthony co-edited *How Do I Begin?: A Hmong American Literary Anthology* (Heyday, 2011), as well as co-edited and co-translated Juan Felipe Herrera's *Akrílica* (Noemi Press, 2022) alongside Carmen Giménez and Farid Matuk. He is a graduate of the MFA-Creative Writing Program at Fresno State where he continues to collaborate with Juan Felipe Herrera and the Laureate Lab Visual Wordist Studio. Anthony has received fellowships from CantoMundo, Community of Writers, and Desert Nights, Rising Stars. He is co-publisher of Noemi Press, a poetry editor for Omnidawn, and is currently faculty in poetry at Randolph College's Low Residency MFA Program. Anthony lives in Fresno, CA with his partner, the poet, Mai Der Vang.

The Rendering
Anthony Cody

Cover art by Phil Chang
"Replacement Ink for Epson Printers (Matte Black 324308) on Hahnemühle Photo Matt
Fibre", 2017, 32.5 x 43.5 in, Unique archival pigment print,
www.philchang.com

Cover and interior set in Arial Black and Adobe Caslon Pro

Cover and interior design by Anthony Cody

Printed in the United States
by Books International, Dulles, Virgina
On 50# Glatfelter B19 Antique
Acid Free Archival Quality Recycled Paper

Publication of this book was made possible in part by gifts from
Katherine & John Gravendyk in honor of Hillary Gravendyk,
Francesca Bell, Mary Mackey, and The New Place Fund

Omnidawn Publishing
Oakland, California
Staff and Volunteers, Spring 2023
Rusty Morrison, senior editor & co-publisher
Laura Joakimson, executive director and poetry & fiction editor
Rob Hendricks, editor of Omniverse, fiction, & poetry, & post-pub marketing
Sharon Zetter, poetry editor & book designer
Liza Flum, poetry editor
Jason Bayani, poetry editor
Anthony Cody, poetry editor
Gail Aronson, fiction editor
Jennifer Metsker, marketing assistant
Jeffrey Kingman, copy editor